OVER 30 YEARS CREATING RESTAURANTS, BARS & HOSPITALITY VENUES WORLDWIDE!

CREATE TO PLATE

Powerful Insights, Strategies & Actions to Create Cutting Edge Hospitality Concepts with Soul

DUNCAN FRASER-SMITH
Voted No.1 Influencer in Caterer Middle East 'POWER 50'

First published by Ultimate World Publishing 2022
Copyright © 2022 Duncan Fraser-Smith

ISBN

Paperback: 978-1-922828-59-0
Ebook: 978-1-922828-60-6

Duncan Fraser-Smith has asserted his rights under the Copyright, Designs and Patents Act 1988 to be identified as the author of this work. The information in this book is based on the author's experiences and opinions. The publisher specifically disclaims responsibility for any adverse consequences which may result from use of the information contained herein. Permission to use information has been sought by the author. Any breaches will be rectified in further editions of the book.

All rights reserved. No part of this publication may be reproduced, stored in or introduced into a retrieval system, or transmitted in any form, or by any means (electronic, mechanical, photocopying, recording or otherwise) without the prior written permission of the author. Any person who does any unauthorised act in relation to this publication may be liable to criminal prosecution and civil claims for damages. Enquiries should be made through the publisher.

Cover design: Ultimate World Publishing
Layout and typesetting: Ultimate World Publishing
Editor: Marinda Wilkinson

Ultimate World Publishing
Diamond Creek,
Victoria Australia 3089
www.writeabook.com.au

DEDICATION

This book is dedicated to two people who have shown unwavering support for me and my journey in this industry over countless years.

To my wife Marlane, who continues to inspire me to live my best and biggest life and has been fundamental in putting this book together. Thank you, my love.

And to the one person who from an early age, always inspired me to be the best man I could be, was there when I was flying high on success as well as when the times got tough. This book is for you.

Thanks Dad.

TESTIMONIALS

Duncan Fraser-Smith is an experienced and astute restaurant operator, food and beverage specialist and accomplished entrepreneurial leader who has greatly influenced and supported my work as a contemporary Middle Eastern chef.

I have known Duncan professionally and personally for over 10 years. He single-handedly steered a very important restaurant, Clé Dubai, bringing me to the city, to an operational stage unseen in Dubai. Opening night was like the opening night at an opera!

Duncan shows great humour and displays the understanding and willingness to share his knowledge, with both his peers and fans. This, along with his caring character, has seen him earn fierce and loyal support amongst the hospitality industry globally.

He is a committed and loyal leader who will always contribute more than expected. He truly gave me the opportunity to shine in a very volatile market, believing in my love of Lebanese cuisine, both contemporary and traditional.

GREG MALOUF, *Modern Middle Eastern Michelin Master*

CREATE TO PLATE

From the outset, Duncan was a valuable and dedicated supporter of The Global Restaurant Investment Forum. His connections and enthusiasm were crucial to its growth, and his extensive industry knowledge and 'black book' were invaluable in gaining support and credibility for the event.

On stage I can always count on Duncan as a moderator and speaker to bring out the best in his guests and deliver an excellent session no matter the circumstances. He was a key figure in driving the development of Dubai's restaurant scene to the next level, particularly in bringing creative, independent operators into the hotel world.

JENNIFER PETTINGER, *Founder, Global Restaurant Investment Forum*

Duncan is a true delight to work with, both personally and professionally. It was my pleasure to work with him at The Cutting Edge Agency and IHG and he has proved his superior F&B knowledge on every occasion.

His enthusiasm, initiative and leadership as a client and as a consultant has resulted in some extremely successful projects. Always willing to do what it takes to deliver his objectives, I would have absolutely no hesitation in recommending Duncan to clients and fellow consultants as he will undoubtably be the most fantastic member of the team.

SARAH-JANE GRANT, *Director/Partner, LXA Interior Design & Architecture*

TESTIMONIALS

Duncan approached us about an idea he had one night – the idea was so pressing he wrote it down on a post-it note and contacted our company the next day. The post-it note simply said: 'MasterChef restaurant'.

MasterChef, the TV Experience restaurant is still operating today in Dubai, having evolved since its first days of opening in the ever-changing culinary world. It would not have come to fruition without Duncan's passion and expertise. As a content production company, known for TV shows such as MasterChef, we are a corporation of creative and commercial people, but not restaurateurs. The talented people who worked with Duncan on bringing MasterChef, the TV Experience to life – the project managers, photographers, former contestants of the show and the brand licensing executives – would not hesitate to work with him again.

Duncan's love for what he does, his ability to jump on a plane and demonstrate how such a TV-inspired restaurant can come to life, made the whole endeavour feel risk and hassle-free. Even the dreaded contracting process, merging brand licensing and the restaurant world, was painless with Duncan. His approach to any kind of bump in the road was professional, business-like, pragmatic and most of all, his passion as an individual in the world of hospitality was infectious. Duncan brought his knowledge of food and dining trends to us and we remain grateful that he helped create the opportunity for people to taste MasterChef dishes for themselves.

BANIJAY GROUP, *formerly Endemol Shine (producers of MasterChef)*

CREATE TO PLATE

Duncan is a truly kind and approachable leader. He has extensive experience in the hospitality industry spanning more than two decades in large hospitality groups internationally. My experience with Duncan as part of my residency in MasterChef, the TV Experience restaurant in Dubai was an unforgettable one. Duncan and his team instantly made me feel at home and like family. They had a good camaraderie and were experts at what they did all under the mentorship of Duncan. I feel lucky to have worked with Duncan on the project and look forward to more opportunities to collaborate in the future.

DIANA CHAN, *MasterChef Australia Champion 2017*

Duncan is one of those people who you meet and immediately know that this guy is on it. I've had the privilege of working with Duncan in Dubai and in Amsterdam, he is refined, succinct and infinitely knowledgeable. One of the very best in the industry, the real deal.

SIMON WOOD, *MasterChef UK Champion 2015, Woods Restaurant Group, UK*

Duncan's expertise and professionalism in the hospitality world are to put it simply, unmatched. Having the pleasure to work with Duncan at MasterChef, the TV Experience in Dubai I realised that his power is not just in his experience but in the way he affects people, bringing out the best of everyone he comes in contact with.

SHAUN O'NEALE, *MasterChef US Champion 2016, Owner Larrea Las Vegas, USA*

TESTIMONIALS

Duncan is conducting thousands of orchestral musicians, at any one time, giving all of them the instruments to thrive at every level, all in order to create a memorable, if not life-changing experience for both his collaborators and his diners.

A world-first restaurant experience ... Duncan says, 'why not'?! He literally brought together MasterChef contestants from around the world so we could be face to face, fork to fork, with the people who make it possible, the passionate foodie viewers.

Duncan is not only the consummate host, but he is in the business of dream building and memory making, for both the people he works with and the diners experiencing his spaces.

From concept to consumer, Duncan's keen attention to detail at every level made the world-first MasterChef restaurant a truly memorable place to experience as a diner and collaborator.

ELENA DUGGAN, *MasterChef Australia Champion 2016*

CREATE TO PLATE

CONTENTS

DEDICATION		iii
INTRODUCTION		1
CHAPTER 1:	IGNITE THE BURNER	3
CHAPTER 2:	UNLOCK YOUR *WHY*	13
CHAPTER 3:	VISION TO CREATION	23
CHAPTER 4:	THE POWER OF INSIGHT	39
CHAPTER 5:	THE ART OF DESIGN	57
CHAPTER 6:	THE HOSPITALITY BIBLE	73
CHAPTER 7:	PASSION VS. PROFIT	87
CHAPTER 8:	HIRE BETTER THAN YOU	105
CHAPTER 9:	LAUNCH PAD TO SUCCESS	117
CHAPTER 10:	YOUR PRESENCE = YOUR PREENT	127
CHAPTER 11:	THE KEYS TO LONGEVITY	139
CHAPTER 12:	LIVING ON THE EDGE	149
THE NEXT STEPS		161
OFFERS		163
SPEAKER BIO		167
RESOURCES		168
ABOUT THE AUTHOR		169

INTRODUCTION

If you've picked up this book with the idea of creating a unique hospitality venue – be it a restaurant, cafe, bar, nightclub, beach club or cocktail lounge – get excited because you've just taken the first step in making it happen!

You may be a chef who has worked in hospitality, but always had a dream to open your own place with your own unique spin. Or, maybe you've been tasked with a project by an investor, owner or operator, to create a new concept or modify an existing outlet to give it a competitive edge.

Whatever your motivation, I look forward to sharing my firsthand experiences and key learnings from creating and launching over 200 hospitality concepts over my 30 year career across the Middle East, Africa, Europe, Asia and Australia.

From a young age, hospitality has been my life. Starting as an ambitious student at Hotel Institute of Management (HIM) Montreux, a top-ranked hotel management school in Switzerland, my passion, enthusiasm and drive for this industry has fast-tracked my career progression. From a young waiter and operations manager in Australia, I advanced to regional and international senior management roles within high profile independent operations as well as 4 & 5 star hotel groups,

CREATE TO PLATE

including Hyatt and InterContinental Hotel Group, and ultimately founded my own business, The Cutting Edge Agency.

My experiences have been vast, working in conjunction with industry experts in the fields of architecture, interior and kitchen design, culinary, marketing, PR, branding and recruitment, in order to provide a comprehensive range of services to owners, investors, hoteliers and homegrown hospitality operators, leading them through every step of the journey from concept vision and creation, through to launch.

My passionate involvement in hospitality initiatives includes my work as a founding member of The Global Restaurant Investment Forum, a moderator of industry panels at conferences, summits and international hospitality events, and a keynote speaker. Recently, I initiated a collaboration with Banijay Group (formerly Endemol Shine), producers of MasterChef, to create and open the world's first 'MasterChef, the TV Experience' restaurant in Dubai.

This book is both a personal account of my practical knowledge and experiences as well as a handbook of powerful insights around the 12 key areas involved in this creative process. You'll learn the strategies and actions required to not only create an industry defining cutting-edge venue, but also incorporate it with 'soul'. This means creating more than just the look – it's also about how the concept makes the guest feel. The human elements of emotional connection have to be created for ultimate success ... that is when the magic of true hospitality happens!

Get ready to be inspired as I support and guide you on your own *EATertainment* journey from **CREATE TO PLATE**!

CHAPTER 1

IGNITE THE BURNER

'Success is not final. Failure is not fatal. It's the courage to continue that counts.'
Winston Churchill

Congratulations on taking the first step towards creating your unique hospitality concept with soul. There's no better way to start than with a fire metaphor when you are going down the path of launching a brand new hospitality venture. So let's get right to it!

Igniting the burner. What am I referring to here? It's that driving force that gets you excited about the project you are about to undertake. There's something truly amazing about walking into a brand new kitchen, turning on the burner for the first time and seeing that blue and yellow flame come to life.

Now, over the last 30 years, I've created more than 200 different types of restaurants, cafes, bars, cocktail lounges and clubs. During this time, I've learnt many different processes and ways to efficiently create and launch a brand new concept, but where it always needs to start is that emotional connecting point, that part in your belly that gets you fired up and excited about what you're about to create. You may have a hundred ideas in your head right now, and that's fantastic. We are going to go through this methodically and carefully to ensure the right outcome, because this industry is unique in so many different ways. Its greatest strength is that we are in the business of making people feel good – in fact, I like to think of it as, the *EATertainment* business!

Through food and drink, we create a relationship with our guests. I call it 'creating concepts with soul' because we have to start from that place within us. We need to find that flame, burning from within, guiding us to launch a venue that has true relevance and authenticity. That is why you are here and why you are reading this book. We're on this journey together.

First things first, a very successful hospitality venue doesn't happen overnight. It is born through thought, process, systems and planning and it lives by execution.

This book lays out a pathway to avoid the pitfalls. There are many things that can distract us or move us off our target in the process of building our hospitality venues. I'm here to give you a useful tool, that you can refer back to, not just now, but for many years to come.

Pursuing something that seems unattainable can be daunting. I know I've had many experiences where I've sat down and looked at the floor plan of an empty building, gazing at the four walls, ceiling and floor and thought, 'What the hell am

I going to put in here?' A hotel's all-day dining restaurant and other similar venues can appear impossible to create and operate successfully. You have to cater for breakfast for a thousand people and then deliver lunch for 150 and still make it into a place that's warm and inviting. There will be times when you look at it and think, it's all too much – but it's at these points that the magic tends to happen. Its not the same for everyone so we will, where appropriate, view our approach from two distinct perspectives:

1. We will view and unpack the keys to creating successful F&B entities from the owner-operator's point of view – you are opening your own venue, and you are the one investing. It's your money and vision.

2. We will also look at this process with the operator only hat on. That's where you are responsible for the creation or re-invention of hospitality venues as the Director of Food and Beverage, the Executive Assistant Manager or Vice President of F&B working within the structure of a larger organisation.

So let's get started on building your concept with soul.

∿

Here we are at the very beginning. There will be obstacles presented and challenges that come up during this journey. However, along the way you will create a well-planned and executed concept with heart that has your DNA imprinted on it. 'Success is not final, and failure is not fatal' so we learn as we go.

CREATE TO PLATE

We can't let our emotions dictate the entire journey. They play a key part in ensuring we build a concept with soul and not just some lifeless box, but we need to keep them in check at the beginning. Fire the excitement, but mindfully.

You will hear me talk a lot about the emotional connectivity within a venue. Some people (not those reading this book) will believe that what we do is simple – secure a venue, add a lick of paint, put some nice lights up, get some music playing, serve good food, create a good atmosphere, offer a nice wine list and mix good cocktails. And that's it. That's, what will work. But no, that's actually only a very small part of the success of businesses like ours.

When creating a concept with soul, let's remember that 'soul' is essentially the emotional and intellectual intensity associated with creativity.

To explain this further, here is an example of how I've executed this in the past. A few years ago, I was asked to come on board and help create a concept that was the second of its kind in the world, called 'Intersect' by Lexus. Now Lexus, as I'm sure many of you know, is a renowned Japanese car brand. The luxury end of the Toyota scale. Words like sophistication, refinement, technology and luxury all come to mind when thinking about this brand – and to top it all off, this specific project was of personal significance to Mr Akio Toyoda himself, the President of the company. I saw it as a very unique opportunity to stretch my approach to concept creation, because how do you generate emotional connectivity with a car in a hospitality venue?

Emotional connectivity is the first lens that you must always look through when creating a restaurant concept. I found it fascinating to sit down and go, right – it's not a car dealership, we're not adding a cafe to a Lexus showroom. We're actually creating a concept that's based on the ethos and the principles of Lexus. Where people can come and spend time and receive amazing hospitality. This was what ignited the burner in me.

It had to be representative of the Lexus brand, but also, provide a hospitality offering that generated an emotional bond with the brand for the guests. As a result, we decided to create a 'third space'. A place between the home and the office where people could come, have a meeting, enjoy super fast wifi, read, have a wine and food experience but with certain elemental touchpoints that were absolutely Lexus specific. The nuances within the venue were such that it didn't scream car, but there were certain strong elements that represented the brand and what Lexus stood for.

I was fortunate to be working with a magnificent design company based out of Japan called Wonderwall, who had very strong design principles around what it was that they wanted to create in this space. I worked very closely with them to make sure that it wasn't over-designed and had elements that made it very warm and inviting and non-car specific. When people walked in, it didn't feel like Lexus was everywhere, but there were certain elements that we created that bridged the crossover. For example, the beautiful bamboo partitioning throughout the venue was very representative of the famous Lexus spindle grill, providing a subtle nod to the vehicle, but again, not overly intrusive and actually fitting in very nicely with the design intention of the venue.

CREATE TO PLATE

In addition, all of the banquette seating in the venue was covered in the leather that had been used in the interior of the LFA supercar, not labelled, not branded, just representative of the brand. A non-obvious connection was being developed. In this way, we were able to take the elements that Lexus represents and put them into a hospitality venue, creating a connection with the guest on a specific level. This was not about selling cars, but about ensconcing guests in the elements that reflect the brand principles. From a food perspective we had a distinctive menu direction for the venue representing the highest quality organic products, including wines and coffees, again reflective of the brand, and giving meaning to our story for the guests. This was where I developed the art of the story, a unique engagement tool that allowed us to open a conversation with the guest. You can't imagine the surprise on their faces when the source of the leather for the banquette was revealed.

The day we opened the door to the venue it felt like it had been lived in for years. It had a real sense of existence. That's the umami of a hospitality venue: having something that is brand new that possesses a lived-in feel on day one.

Ask yourself – how is my venue going to make people feel when they walk through the door?

That's the essence of its soul.

The fire within

Understanding how you want people to feel in your venue, makes your inner flame burn brighter. At this stage you probably have a gut feeling as to the type of venue you want to create. Be it a rockstar wine bar, an amazing distillery, or a high-end French bistro, I'm sure you've got that feeling already. Now we need to build it and stoke it.

For the operators out there, let's put on our Director of Food and Beverage hats for a moment and assume that the hotel General Manager or the owning company has come to us and said, 'we've got this space'.

This did happen to me. It was a meeting room and the owning company wanted me to repurpose it as a F&B venue because they thought it would generate a better return for the property. Fantastic! Here was my opportunity to shine. I'm going to show the corporate office and the owning company just what I can do. My fire was lit and through many of the steps that follow throughout this book, I created a cafe, on steroids! Coffee and cakes during the day and a wine bar at night. Truly the best of both worlds. I understood that there is no limit to creativity for a hospitality concept.

CREATE TO PLATE

Recently, my wife and I created our own restaurant brand based on how we felt during the amazing dining experiences that we'd had on our travels to the Mediterranean during our summer vacations. We wanted to re-create specific elements in our venue, that would connect our guests with these feelings, tastes and ambience as well as evoke their own memories of a European summer vacation. And so, our fire was lit ... and 'Vesper Bistro and Bar' was born.

We had some great Mediterranean restaurants in very close proximity to our proposed location in the neighbourhood, but they were either purely French, Italian, Spanish, Turkish or Greek. We needed to augment and differentiate our concept by harnessing one element that was not well represented but had an amazing way of connecting with everyone.

That element was the Mediterranean islands. Think about it for a second. You've got all of France, Italy, Greece and Spain very well represented in the dining market, but what about the likes of Corsica, Corfu, Sardinia, Capri, Mykonos, Santorini or Majorca?

Where could you go and experience an authentic Corsican dish or Madeiran bacalao in one venue? These islands have unique cuisines and dishes attributable to them that resonated with our guests, conjuring the feeling of taking 'their palate on vacation'.

When people think of islands or any island holiday, it generally creates an emotional connection attached to pleasurable memories. We knew that we were in the memory making business as well and this ignited our motivation!

The key to your success will rely 100 per cent on you and your involvement and commitment to see this through your own fire within.

You may be asking yourself at this stage, what if I don't know where to start? It's okay to feel a little overwhelmed. We are going to walk through the process together. There is a starting point and you are there right now. The fact that you have ignited the burner at this stage is the beginning.

Your next question may be, what if I can't dedicate the time?

Hospitality operations are living, breathing entities and we must find the time to nurture and support them. If you view this as a vehicle for creating and spreading joy, then time must be dedicated to it because you are creating an experience for others. You will bring joy into people's lives. They are coming to be impacted on a level that plays with and enhances their emotional experience. And so time is definitely something you'll find. Just like you're doing now by reading this.

If you are saying to yourself that, 'I trust my gut, no-one can teach me otherwise', well, that is great! This process is not about ignoring your gut instincts. Far from it! Think of it as a way to keep your gut in check. It's like a sense check. Shall we continue?

CREATE TO PLATE

ACTION

Free Hospitality Concept 50-Point Checklist
(See RESOURCES page back of the book)

This checklist will help you identify the stages, timelines and actions that you need to consider before opening a hospitality venue.

SLAM DUNK!

'In the beginning, it's so important to light the fire for the project. You may not know where to channel that energy yet but be sure that fire is burning brightly.'

CHAPTER 2

UNLOCK YOUR *WHY*

'People don't buy what you do, they buy why you do it.'
Simon Sinek

Why do you really want to do this? You really need to turn the camera around and look deep within yourselves to answer this question. So understanding *why* you are here is important before we move any further. What are your motivations and drivers? We need to understand first: is the motivation purely money and profit? Are you creating this because at the end of the day, you want to make a ton of money out of it?

If the answer is yes, GREAT! There's nothing wrong with that. Some people do approach hospitality purely with financial gain as their driver. Understanding that now will change your approach to developing your concept going forward.

Perhaps your motivation is ego. You want to build restaurants, bars and clubs, based on satisfying your ego. You want to be able to say, 'I've got a restaurant, come and hang out in my bar.' You want your friends to come and see your venue because it's a status symbol of your success. That's justifiable, if it is successful. Will it be successful? We'll get to that a little later on.

You may be tasked with it, by an owning company or the head of operations, and I'm talking specifically here to our F&B Managers, Directors of F&B and Executive Assistant Managers in large corporate operations. They've said, 'We need you to go and create this restaurant.' Even if you have been given the challenge, you still need to understand *why* you are excited by it, or not excited by it, whatever the case may be.

Right now you may be asking, *why* do I need to know this? Creating a hospitality venue is a hugely personal undertaking. There are touchpoints and elements – from a wall fabric to a carpet to the way a menu is designed – that all have a personal touch to them heavily driven by your input. You've got to understand from the start how much of those elements you want to do yourself, then work out *why* is it that you want to take those specific touchpoints on. If it's just because you've always wanted to, then your passion is driving the journey. You're fulfilling your desire, because you've always dreamed of doing it. You might have been an accountant for the last 30 years or so, a doctor or a dentist, and your secretly harboured desire was to have a little coffee shop on the corner of the local high street with the best single origin beans available in town. Maybe this is the moment when you've thought, 'to heck with it, I've been passionate about doing this for years and I'm doing it now'.

Clarity on your *why* is key

Did you know that many people open restaurants and bars without being clear on *why* they did it? They forge ahead because they know they want it, but then when the numbers don't come in, they start to panic. When opening a venue, change is a given and with change comes more expense, so knowing *why* you are doing it upfront is crucial. If you look at yourself and say, 'I've been given a budget of a couple hundred grand to create a new venue and don't really know *why*,' then STOP RIGHT NOW! Check yourself and go back to looking at what it is that ignites your burner. Following this process sets you up for executing something truly unique with a foundation for success.

Understanding *why* you are doing it, be it ego, money, passion, profit or because you were tasked with the challenge, sets up the way that you'll approach how to do it. The key to success is clarity. It's not about the product that you've created. It's actually more about *why* have you created it and *why* your customers are going to be invested in what you've done.

Conversely, going through the motions without clarity on the motivation can result in business failure. The *why* establishes the vision. In one of our upcoming chapters we look at establishing the vision, which is then shared across your team. If the *why* is unclear, so too is the team in knowing how to execute it.

We want to unlock your purpose for opening, creating or reinventing this venue. What are your inner motivations and what can be done to keep them aligned? It's critical to keep this front of mind so you can stay on track, stay focused and stay true to your direction. What drives you to be in this industry? What about it feeds your soul?

It's very easy to deviate from the course when your *why* is not a solid foundation. *Why* are you opening an American smokehouse in the Marina area? *Why* are you doing that? *Why* do you feel that it is important for the area? And *why* are your guests and colleagues going to buy into it?

Stay true to your path

The reason we focus on the *why* so much during this early stage is to stay true to the vision – because what invariably happens in the formation stages of any hospitality business is influence.

You're going to be influenced by people with ideas that may be contrary to yours. These can be friends, family, peers … even your accountant will have an opinion! 'You've got such a great space and I'm loving the Indian curry theme but can I suggest you put in a mobile hot dog stand in the back of the room because I love hot dogs?' These influences will make you question your *why*. Remember, *why* is your reason for creating this venue so don't let others push you off track.

What happens when you question your *why*? You might say, 'I'm doing this because I'm so passionate about it, but then they're telling me I'm not going to make any money. And they're telling me that the design isn't great and they're telling me that they think I should be doing a coffee shop instead of a wine bar.' This is just noise; acknowledge them, and then stay true. It keeps you on a path.

UNLOCK YOUR WHY

A key learning over the last 30 years is that when you stray off that path and let outside influences come in and water down your core belief structure as to *why* you're doing this, you've got a greater propensity for failure. This has happened to me on several occasions.

So, back yourself 100%.

To those owner operators out there who are going into this and saying, 'It's my money that I'm putting in, and this is what I want to do and here are the three reasons *why* I want to do it,' back yourself and stay true. Don't be persuaded off your path.

Make sure your belief structure on *why* you are doing it is rock solid. If you're doing it for profit and for money, because you've done a financial model that says you're going to make BIG dollars, fantastic!

Maybe you've got squillions of dollars already, and you want to have it as a halo project? Don't let people talk you out of it. Further down the track, you might question your motivations if it's not making any money, but don't let others put questions in your head. This is the hospitality industry and at the end of the day, we should all be motivated by a driving force to execute amazing experiences for our guests. End of story!

For all the C-level managers or directors in larger organisations, it's essential you get the buy-in of your key stakeholders. Maybe you already understand your *why*. Perhaps you've been given a beautiful footprint of real estate to develop for a hospitality concept, and you have a real gut feeling for what needs to go in that space. You may say to yourself, 'I've been in this hotel for three years and I know what the people want. I know the experience they want to have is an artisanal bakery and this is what I'm going to put forward.' With that mindset, your gut instinct tells you the people want this. In this case, you need to get the buy-in from your key stakeholders.

There are two important reasons for doing this. Firstly, because you are going to steer them in the direction you want to go. Secondly, you need to solidify your ideas, so your vision remains true. This is crucial, particularly in large organisations, as personnel changes can happen, and the people you are working with now, may or may not be there through the creation stage and beyond.

A simple tool I use to eradicate any miscommunication in this situation, is a one-page ideation slide. Now, this is a visually impactful slide that you get your key stakeholders, your General Manager, your corporate Director of Operations or your owner, to sign off on at the start. This gives you security, that your intention, your purpose, your driving force, your *why* is protected, and it's not going to be overridden or changed.

I've worked for quite a few large international hotel groups and without mentioning names, there have been times where I have been three quarters of the way through developing a project that I was hugely passionate about and all the key stakeholders had bought into it, and then it was thrown into chaos. At the beginning, everyone was aligned and the concept itself was taking shape. Suddenly a new Vice President of corporate F&B (not based in my office) comes in, and proclaims, 'I don't like that. Let's go in a different direction Duncan. It's not really, what I want.'

Because I didn't have everyone's signatures on a document or proof that it had all been confirmed by the 'powers that be', we got derailed. Did we come up with another concept? Yes. Was it as good as the first one? No. Did it survive? No. A key point to remember here, is that when you're working for a large organisation, as a Director of F&B or even a corporate level designer, it's essential to have a critical moment in the development phase where your ideation is locked in and signed off.

Another example of a potential issue is when owners and operators have opposing views. The operator may say, 'I know exactly what we're going to do with the all-day dining restaurant.' (*Why* = serve guests breakfast, lunch and dinner.) But the owner states, 'No, you're not, because I want a seafood restaurant.' (*Why* = halo.) 'But we're in the middle of the desert?' you might respond. But they stick firm, replying, 'I understand, but I want a seafood restaurant.'

These scenarios come up regularly. As an operator, it is your role to influence the owner in the direction that you believe is going to be most successful. The owner is paying you a fee through your hotel management or restaurant management contract. You are being paid because of your expertise. The operator is making their decision based on money, financial ROI, and the owner is wanting a seafood restaurant because of his/her ego. Guess who won that one? Understanding the *why* motivations are critical!

A simple strategy to keep you aligned and on track is scheduling set times to work on your creative project. We get distracted a lot. It's part of human nature. If this is your first or only project, then you're likely very dedicated to it and you don't have an issue with time. You've got to create one izakaya dining room. Great! Then you can dedicate your time and focus to that. However, if you're already running multiple established venues, then you have to block time out in your day to be able to focus on *why* you are creating this new concept.

Perhaps you need music, a quiet space and to have your phone on silent during that period of time. I know when I was working at IHG, we used to have dedicated rooms where you could go and be creative. A small cubicle where you could sit down and noise was virtually non-existent. That was where you could get creative and lock in your ideation slide without being distracted, or influenced by anyone else. Then get it signed off by your stakeholders of course!

Remember, backing yourself instils confidence in others that you do know what you're talking about and you are a master of your chosen craft (i.e. concept creation with soul). This is the key to your future success.

So, how about those who say, 'I'm just doing this, because its my job'? If that's how you really feel, then maybe this isn't the right industry for you. This is a real opportunity for amazing creative expression. But if you are thinking from the start about going with a concept that you tried five years ago, at another property somewhere and repurposing that, you are setting yourself up for failure. Instead, look at it as an opportunity to test yourself, learn something new and develop skills that you may not have had a chance to try yet. Most people don't have the opportunity to sit back with a blank sheet of paper and create a concept from scratch.

It's very rare that these opportunities present themselves. I had just graduated from hotel management school in Switzerland back in the mid-90s and had returned to Australia to start working for Hyatt. Within 12 months, I'd moved from Melbourne to Sydney to work on the redevelopment of the Hyatt Kingsgate, which was transitioning to the Hyatt Regency, Sydney. I was fortunate to be heavily involved in the concepting of the new restaurant called Xu. I was in my early twenties and I'd never done this before. I had the opportunity to work with all of the different stakeholders to come up with a concept that actually was brand new for, firstly the Australian market, and subsequently, Hyatt's global platform.

We were the first restaurant ever with an open kitchen in the group's portfolio. In addition we broke with tradition and had our team members on the floor with earrings, tattoos and men with facial hair. This seems normal now, but breaking those barriers and boundaries, on my first ever concept creation was just phenomenal. And that was the first time I discovered how important soul and personality is to an outlet.

Some of you might be saying, 'I don't care about profit. I just want a bar that's mine.' Let me challenge you by saying you might not care about profit now. And I have numerous examples of people that have told me that they want all the fixtures to be done in gold and Lalique crystal in the bathrooms, because it's theirs and they want it to showcase a certain level of wealth, blah blah blah. But at the end of the day, it's a business, and a business needs to have an ROI.

If you don't set it up for success at the outset, with a thorough understanding of *why* you're doing it, you're going to look back and say, 'Hang on a second, I'm just pouring money in here and I'm not getting anything back.' You might not care about profit now, but if it doesn't work, then you'll need to invest to change it. Or perhaps, sell it to another, who then needs to change it. Even if this journey for you is purely ego driven, *why* wouldn't you make it as successful as you can? That's what this book is about. Establishing your business with the best possible tools to give you success from the day you open the doors.

ACTION

Complete a one-page concept ideation slide for your ideal/dream concept.
(See RESOURCES page back of book)

SLAM DUNK!

'Truly understanding why you are opening a venue in the hospitality world sets up different approaches as to how you should do it. Clarity is key.'

CHAPTER 3

VISION TO CREATION

'Good restaurant designers are about achieving equilibrium between the food service and design, in effect telling a complete story.'
David Rockwell

So by now you've got the juices flowing. Your mind is full of ideas. You're thinking, 'I can do this! I can do that! And wow, how good is that going to look? I want to have beers on tap, a wall full of wine, mosaic tiles on the floor …' You're being flooded with ideas.

This is the creative stage, where you are completely unrestricted in your thoughts and you get to pull the best pieces out of your imagination and start to make them real. We are going to take all of those amazing thoughts and feelings and actually move them into the concept stage.

In this chapter we cover that transition.

CREATE TO PLATE

This is the part I have the most fun with on every concept that I create. It allows creativity to come out of the mind and onto the paper. The name of the book 'Create to Plate' comes from this stage, where we start to plate up our creativity. We put it on a dish, play with the ingredients and look at how it presents itself. It really is the first tangible piece of the project. And some would say the most important, because at the end of this process, you will have some amazing tools that help you leverage and best maximise the concept.

You've got all of these wonderful ideas going around in your head, now is the time to take them and put them down into a concept brief. This is where you capture all the relevant elements of the concept in order. Rather than jumping from what sort of kitchen you want to what sort of bar you want, there is a step-by-step process to follow, to make sure that nothing is missed out.

This is where you get to really lock in the direction of your concept. You will learn the value of mood boards. I'm sure a lot of you have played with things like Pinterest, where you are web surfing and saying, 'WOW, I'd love that chair in my forever house, I'll put that on there.' Or, 'I've always wanted to go to Brazil' and you drop an image of Rio De Janiero's Copacabana Beach on there for inspiration. That's a mood board.

The mood board and your concept's soul is very much the same thing. It is where you stand back and look at the imagery that inspires you based on your creative direction. Placing these look and feel images in front of you allows you to begin building a concept brief based on authenticity and relevance.

VISION TO CREATION

I've seen it time and time again, when people rush into a project because they've signed a lease and will be paying money and they just want to be open. 'Let's get the doors open, let's get things happening, put a kitchen in there, put the chef in, put the bar manager in and let's just get it going.' But they have not created a concept brief and things get missed.

Can you believe it? I have seen projects in the past in which a bar has been built, the most beautiful bar finished in lava stone, in a nightclub where mixology based cocktails were to be the stand-out feature. Absolutely amazing design. What was missed I hear you ask? Ice wells. There were no ice wells for the ice to be placed behind the bar. Costly error that should have been captured during concept creation.

The process of building your concept brief involves highlighting your unique selling points (USPs) and essential pieces of equipment (e.g. ice wells!!!) in order to execute your operation. Taking the time to complete this process, eradicates the chance of costly omissions from occurring.

In another example, a brand new, stunning French provincial cafe, serving the most amazing macarons, biscuits and patisserie opened. It was only small, 30 seats, but a truly exquisite space. The operator had invested thousands of dollars on their USP, an extremely intricate coffee machine that stood proudly in the centre of the jewel-like display cabinets. However, the coffee machine's capacity required 3-phase power. There was no provision for 3-phase power when they came to connect it. They were forced to lose their intricate machine and settle for a more 'standard' 2 Grup one because they hadn't looked at the specifications in their planning stages. It was in their concept brief, but the requirements for it were overlooked.

One final example that illustrates the need to approach your wishes and desires with a touch of reality was a concept created around fire. The feature of the kitchen was an all gas, charcoal and natural woodfired cooking line. It had gas burners, gas fryers, wood ovens and even a wok station. The owner had originally designed the concept for a different location but found another that he preferred and so decided to insert his concept brief into the new location. Easy, yes? No.

When this beautiful equipment arrived at the new site, the owner discovered that the property was provisioned for electrical and induction cooking only. No GAS OR EXPOSED FLAME! Moral of this story is, no matter how perfect your concept brief is, it may need revisions based on the location's capabilities.

The step-by-step creative process

Remember, we are in the storytelling business – our restaurants, our bars, our outlets, our hospitality venues are all there to tell a story. Every single element that comes into play forms part of that story – the beginning, the middle and the end, hopefully with not too many villains popping up to disrupt things along the way. That is the beauty of this creative process: we get to nail down the fundamentals of our story.

Failing to follow a process like this, that is tried and true, can leave you with a venue that is disjointed, non-communicative, and subsequently, empty. We want to ensure that your story is cohesive. So, this process of building a concept brief is the cohesion. It's the gel that brings all of your ideas together in one unified form where we can look at it in a five to ten page document and get a really good understanding of exactly what you are creating, what you're serving, how you're serving it, what you're serving it with, who's serving it and where it's being prepared.

To help explain the creative process, I'll use a real-life example. At the end of the book, you can download this exact example for your records.

So, let's now unpack the concept brief, and explore the different steps involved in the creative process which include:

- Crafting a concept statement
- Pinpointing the USPs that set you apart
- Choosing words to describe the look and feel
- Describing the furniture, fixtures and equipment
- Establishing the menu/cuisine direction
- Defining the service style and touchpoints
- Exploring your brand ideas

Crafting a concept statement

So, let's start with the concept statement. This is the short, but powerful concise summary of the vision, mission and values of the concept. It can be broken down into an elevator pitch that discusses the DNA of the concept. Most importantly, it engages others on that emotive level. What do I get when I am there? How does it feel? Is there somewhere I may know that gives me that same feeling?

CREATE TO PLATE

The example venue we are using to create our concept brief is a New Orleans smokehouse and bar. What do I mean by a New Orleans smokehouse and bar?

Here's the concept statement:

> 'The smokehouse is a stylised restaurant bar and lounge that offers classic American smoked meats with an assortment of traditional American homage dishes. It features a lounge setting by day and transforms into a club-style setting for the evenings.
>
> This space is a truly unique outlet set to position itself as an unpretentious, yet sophisticated venue known for its crafted, innovative, smoked meat offering.'

You see that in the above statement I'm using language and vocabulary, to convey to my stakeholders and my audience, the style and the ambience of a place to eat, drink and socialise, for simple everyday affairs and stylish occasions. We're painting a picture that it is multifaceted. A simple lunch during the day, or come in the evenings for an elevated experience inspired by the essence of New Orleans.

Having read this now, my thoughts go towards, this being 'a perfect opportunity to work with a creative, inspiring New Orleans chef who understands the core service and product.'

What I've done there, is introduce the potential of bringing in a chef or pitmaster from New Orleans to come onboard and oversee the operation. This would all be on the first slide of the concept brief, to give people a taste of what is to come.

Pinpointing the USPs that sets you apart

Next, I ask myself the key question: what is my USP *(Unique Selling Point)* going to be? 'The Smoker!' This is a quintessential part of the cooking methodology that can be a USP in the venue.

Where does the smoker sit? Is it encased in a glass room, in the heart of the venue that is visible for everyone to see? Does it sit outside on a terrace? Will it be a USP that people want to take photos with and share on social? The smoker permeates the air with a distinct aroma, engaging everyone's senses and setting you up for the meal yet to come. Now I hope your mouth is watering, because it is super important for people to be seeing, feeling and tasting the concept.

This brief we are discussing here is for a fictional smokehouse. In real life, I created a smokehouse concept called The Blacksmith which actually did have a smoker called Old Betty, and Old Betty actually lived on the first floor terrace of the restaurant and was a huge visual cue to what we were doing. People could see it when driving down the street. They could see Old Betty smoking away on the terrace. Initially we were going to have all the smokers inside the building, but when that wasn't going to be feasible, Putting Old Betty on the balcony was the best thing that we could possibly have done.

Choosing words to describe the look and feel

Your brief should be literally talking to the concept, so now we want to choose words to bring it to life. How does it feel when you sit in there? What is the generic menu offering going to be? How does it work? Does it feel like a smokehouse? I usually use three words that instantly describe the ambience of the venue. For this smokehouse, featuring the smoker, I would use: 'Masculine, Assertive and Theatrical.'

Thinking about a New Orleans smokehouse with a visible smoker in the room summed up with the words: masculine, assertive and theatrical, you start to build a picture in your mind of what this will look like. Remember the sky is the limit when putting down all of your desires and wishes for the concept, shaping it and framing it in a document that can be handed to interior designers, owners and other consultants.

There are no actual pictures yet so we need to describe in words how the environment is going to feel. Bullet points work well here to separate each idea.

Here's what I imagine for our smokehouse:

- 'Inspired by the legendary great smokehouses of New Orleans. This restaurant will be a modern version of the original.' Taking the past and twisting it into today.
- 'Semi-private dining room with cleverly designed partitions, allowing guests to view activities in the main dining room.' Painting the image of separation within the venue. It's not a hall, it's not a massive open space. Guests from those private dining areas will be able to see what's happening in the main dining room and the smoker at the same time.
- 'Tables and chairs to be designed and positioned in a way that each one enjoys the view with booths

and banquettes to augment the space.' The aspect might be the view of the room, or you might have 180 degree windows around your environment. You need to maximise your seating, so that people get the benefit of the views that you have available.
- 'Warm colour tones and ambient lighting.' No harsh lighting. We're not talking fluorescent or neon. We're talking warmth, no light is direct or hitting the table in a harsh way.
- 'Timber and warm leather upholstery to give a sense of solidity and tradition.' People reading this will immediately feel that the seating elements will be solid and comfortable.
- 'Dry aging cabinet display.' Meats that are going through the aging process are visible to the guests.
- 'An elegant bar with a backlit display.' Maybe there is a little 1920s influence in the space?
- 'Music area with stage and relevant fittings for a three-piece jazz band.' This example is a bit of a wishlist item, as I may or may not be able to fit it into the space, but when I'm thinking about my New Orleans smokehouse concept, it is something I would like.

Describing the furniture, fixtures and equipment

The next considerations are the FF&E *(furniture, fixtures and equipment)* and the OS&E *(operating supplies and equipment)*. We covered a little of this in our description above, so use that as inspiration to write a more detailed list of what you will need. Keep in mind, you may need to revisit this step after you have defined your service style to be sure it all aligns.

CREATE TO PLATE

We want to create a masculine space with some feminine touches such as comfortable arm chairs and banquettes, with a mix of square and round tables. Understand what type of tables to have in your space for the greatest flexibility, but also to cater for large guests and large group bookings. I can see cast-iron side dishes, sturdy and contemporary glassware with a retro feel, beautiful coupes with etched crystal and a purpose designed and built gueridon for tableside service, finished with a simple tabletop candle and single fresh flower for decoration.

Establishing the menu/cuisine direction

Now is the time to establish a menu direction, the type of cuisine you'll offer, making sure that it's a perfect fit with the design and style of the restaurant. The menu direction for this concept is focused on beef from the great cattle rearing nations across the globe, such as Argentina, Scotland, Australia, South Africa and the USA. Seafood and poultry will be sourced under the same guidance offering only the highest quality categories on the menu.

Now I'm not a chef, I never professed to be a chef, but I do know food, so for a New Orleans-style smokehouse, what would I want to have on my menu? Here are some of the dishes I can imagine:

- Colossal shrimp cocktail with classic tomato horseradish dip
- Seabass ceviche with yuzu and pomelo
- Black Angus bresola
- Tartar with quail's egg

- Carpaccio with truffle oil
- Hickory-smoked milk-fed veal (27 weeks)
- Oak-smoked farmed chicken
- Maple-smoked Kobe beef brisket
- Birch-smoked eggplant

(Remembering to cater for our vegetarian and vegan people.)

The drinks direction we're talking will feature:

- Fresh pressed juices
- High-end bottle tonics and mixers
- Housemade syrups, bitters and infusions
- Mixology and cocktails
- Artisanal wines
- Beer offerings

Remember, at this point, I still have no name. I have no brand at this stage. Right now, we are just creating a concept.

Defining the service style and touchpoints

Next we need to define our service style and service direction. What are the key signature moments in service that people are going to experience?

Moment 1: Warm bread selection to be served while guests are looking at the menu. Tick! (Who doesn't love warm bread and butter.)

Moment 2: Tomahawk steaks will be presented on a wooden board shown to guests, then cut and served in front of them.

CREATE TO PLATE

Moment 3: Introduce table service. Caesar salad, dressed and tossed in front of guests.

Additional key service approaches would include:

- offer freshly ground pepper as a condiment, not left on the table
- a homemade truffle delicacy served after the bill is presented
- a signature parting gift presented at the closing of service (relish is always good)
- every element of each drink is handmade from freshly squeezed juices through to spritzers and dehydrated garnishes

So these are the little touchpoints which will leave a lasting impression on our guests. The service style is knowledgeable, every service person will understand the menu, specials and story behind the venue. They understand the chef's style and philosophy, and most importantly, the difference in the cuts of meat. As to how the dishes are to be executed and the tableside engagements, it's professional and energetic, with continuous interaction with guests and a true sense of pride and ownership in the venue.

Now, with the above mapped out, you can specify the type of uniforms you want. Do you want black trousers? Do you want aprons? Do you want classic white chef coats for kitchen staff? The bar staff are impeccable and wearing modern vests and thin ties.

Exploring your brand ideas – mood boards

So we now have the outline of a concept brief.

To visualise this further, we must bring our mood board to life, by sourcing imagery from the web, magazines, even personal photographs, to further build the look and feel of your venue and begin to define your brand.

What are some of the key elements that we need to put into this venue?

You've seen, through the concept brief, how I talk about unique selling points or USPs and your mood board should centre around these. They are the little elements that trigger moments that become memorable for guests. A memory is triggered by an emotion, and so when someone feels happy, it embeds a bookmark in that memory. Having these little wow moments throughout the guests' journey intensifies those experiences.

Don't be afraid to use the internet and populate as many images as you can for your mood board. They will not all necessarily make it into the concept document but what you have left over can potentially be used for your next venture.

If you are working with third parties such as celebrity chefs, or chefs that are absolutely phenomenal in their particular lane of culinary execution, or you wish to work with them, put them on your mood board. Putting it on there makes it tangible. I have been fortunate to work with some amazing Michelin starred chefs, and I've had the great fortune to do that because the project felt right, and I wanted them to be a part of it. So put it all out there. It's not real until it's real.

Your concept brief sets you up for success

The resisters amongst you will look at this again and say 'Oh my goodness, how much time will it take to do all of these steps? It's a lot to do and I just want to get my place up and running.'

The reason I share this sample concept brief with you is this. Investing the time in doing this at this early stage of your concept is going to save you a lot of additional time and headaches in the future. It's far better to do this now, before you're up and running, so that you can then execute it with finesse and authenticity. Lock this down and you'll have a concept brief that has a lot of flesh, a lot of meat on the bone.

Concepting gives you a really good understanding of what you're doing. Investing the time in it right now is priceless in helping you succeed. Now, some of you may be sitting there and saying, I don't know a thing about kitchen or bar requirements, and that's absolutely fine. I am not a barista or bartender by trade. I'm not a chef: I am a restaurateur. Fortunately, there are many people out there that specialise in these areas and partnering with them, working with them, depending on the scale and size of your venue, is an investment that will contribute to your overall success.

There are resources out there to assist you with space planning your kitchen and bar and to help you work on the layouts of your areas. Additionally, if you're struggling to think of anything unique about your concept, I'm here to tell you that the great news is, what's unique about your concept right now is YOU. You may have been inspired by others, and now you have an idea. You understand what it is, you understand why you're doing it and now you're putting it down. This is your unique piece. You've created this. Can you imagine the feeling you will have on the first night of opening? What is the one thing that you want all of your guests to talk about?

With the smokehouse example, I would want them talking about the beautiful fabrics on the banquette, the smoker in the venue and the magnificent steaks that we have available. It can be anything from the presentation of a 1.5 kilogram Tomahawk steak to an Instagrammable wall in a venue.

When I launched Masterchef, the TV Experience in 2019, and the 'M' Swirl logo went up on the wall, how many people came in to take a photo in front of it for that instagrammable moment? Hundreds. Initially we had a table underneath it, but learned quickly that it needed to be moved so we could have people stand underneath it and get their photo taken. We maximised our USP there.

I can't tell you how many times I've gotten into my car to go to an opening of one of my venues, and every time, I've always taken a moment to reflect on the fact that when I come back to my car at the end of the evening, that venue will be open. To acknowledge that this living, breathing, entity that I have spent months, or even years, creating will actually have a life of its own after that evening. It's a wonderful feeling.

CREATE TO PLATE

ACTION

Create a one-page mood board for your concept. Download the sample concept brief for the New Orleans smokehouse *(See RESOURCES page back of book)*

SLAM DUNK!

'This is the most important part of the process because getting your ideas down into a cohesive document is the first step in turning your thoughts into living things.'

CHAPTER 4

THE POWER OF INSIGHT

'Creativity is intelligence having fun.'

Albert Einstein

When launching any new product into the marketplace, the first thing you want to know is will anyone buy it? Over the following pages, you'll uncover some insights that will address this question, and guarantee you lay a foundation for success from the outset.

First up is market intelligence.

Why is it so important? It gives us an edge over our competitors, ultimately, but more importantly, it allows us to see and understand what other businesses are doing in the areas that you are going to be competing in. Now, this is not just necessarily about the same type of concept that you are doing. If you are opening a bar, pub or nightclub, this is not just about looking at all the other bars, pubs and nightclubs in the area.

This is about understanding your local market as a whole, and why local guests are going out. What gets them out of the door? What makes them go and part with their hard-earned dollars in these venues? Understanding your local market, and competitor-set is hugely important.

You will deep dive into similar existing concepts in the area. If you are wanting to open a Japanese tatami room or a Thai restaurant or a seafood bar then it's pertinent to look at who else in the area is already doing that. They may not be exactly the same, but have similar characteristics, so that you can have a really good understanding of why people are going to go out to these venues. How many people in the area will say of an evening 'I want Japanese, here are the five choices I've got,' and you, as a new outlet, need to be one of them.

What are others offering? What is in the market there? What are their price points? How do they structure their menus? Do they do a set menu? Do they do it course by course, entrée, main, dessert? Is it shared? Where do your potential guests go and why? Who are they? Are you purely targeting the local community or further afield?

Targeting your local community can be a fantastic approach. I remember working with IHG in developing their Hotel Indigo concept, where the restaurant is created in each property with the neighbourhood it sits in at the heart of the hotel and its offerings. This taps into and becomes very relevant in the markets that they operate in.

Maybe that is where you want to play. Maybe you want to be a diner or bar that is purely there to cater to the needs of the locals in your area. Are you planning on targeting interstate or international visitors too? Do you expect your advertising to roll out in the Qantas or Emirates magazine? Are you going to be a tourist-focused operation? Are they potential guests for you? Are people going to arrive in the city or country that you're in and know that one of the top five restaurants that they need to go to is yours? Market insights help you know that people, now, do make travel decisions based on, believe it or not, gastronomic journeys and dining destinations.

Understanding who your potential guests are and how you're going to reach them, communicate with them and engage them, allows you to then create your customer profile around them. The customer profile is a snapshot of who is the ideal potential person coming into your venue. For example, my regular weekly customer demographic is aged 25 to 40. They dine out three times a week. They don't spend a lot when they go out, but they go out regularly. They work in the fashion, accounting or freelance fields.

Finally, market insight will also give you an understanding of the type of awards that have been won by venues in your area, and a clearer understanding of which of those awards you want to compete in.

Now, it's not to say you have to compete, but if there are restaurants in your market that are similar concepts to yours and have won awards, let's find out why they won. What is it that people have said about them? What have the critics said about these restaurants that makes them award-winning? Maybe you have Michelin or Gault Millau in your city? What is differentiating a one-hat from a three-hat outlet in your area?

Building an understanding of this market intelligence gets you into a position to launch something that is ultimately highly relevant to your potential guests. The more you can dig into who your market is, who your customer base is and why they go out, the greater chance you have of launching a restaurant into the market that is relevant at that time. Unless your intention is to literally be everything to everyone (note: I do not recommend this approach), this process can introduce you to your perfect guests before your doors are even open.

As a result of your market intelligence and establishing your customer profile, you will refine your offering in order to make sure that you are 100% relevant and authentic to the requirements of the potential guests to your venue. Imagine what it would be like competing in a world where everyone else knows more about your customer than you do. Think about being a high-performing athlete competing at the Olympic Games, and you don't know anything about your competition. You've done no research into their strengths, their weaknesses, what they do, how they do it, why they hit certain targets, where they are making up the most time in their particular lap or race.

Having those insights gives you an advantage over people that don't, and that contributes to your blueprint for success.

Gathering your data

Your competitor set (comp-set), are the businesses that are competing with you for guests. They may not be the same cuisine or location or have the same offering, but when people are choosing to go out, they are considered with you at the same time. Never underestimate the power of your concept if you want your potential guests spending money in your place not the one next door. You need to know their wishes. What drives them? What are their pain points? You need to understand this to deliver exceptional hospitality.

Imagine a guest walks out the door with an assumption in their head about how much they're willing to spend on a particular night. The rest of the decision-making process could come down to how a place feels, how a place looks, how they've been treated before, whether they've been recommended, etc. Let's say, $500 is what they're prepared to spend on this night out. Every restaurant in your comp-set is competing for that $500, especially if they've made a booking with you. It's your offering and what you produce that will give you the edge to ensure that your guests, firstly, walk through the door for the first time, and then become loyal and repeat customers in the future.

So the big question is, how do you get all this information? How do you get this insight and get this understanding? Yes, there are people that can source it and do the legwork for you. But I've found in the past that, especially in certain projects, understanding your market by doing the research yourself is considerably more advantageous than outsourcing it. There are two ways to do this. If time is an issue, simply google it! Searching on Google is a great way to generate market insight. Alternatively, you can deep dive, and develop a highly detailed market research report. I will showcase how to do this and a sample will be available to download at the back of the book.

For now, let's look at a simple online search. For this example, we'll use the city of Sydney, Australia, and assume you are planning to open a new Italian trattoria. You google Italian restaurants in your area, and then you'll see the top ones will pop up, with some reviews. You're able to pull together the shape of the restaurant and how it's perceived in the marketplace. That's quite an easy way to get started.

Deep impact market research is valuable and provides you with an enormous amount of insight into areas that you may not have thought about. Or if you are coming into a new property, especially those operators with multiple venues, it provides insight into gaps in the market and assists with expanding into new regions.

In addition, if you have moved regions, cities or even properties, detailed market research is a really good snapshot to have as a tool. Don't be daunted by the fact that these things can be 60 pages long. Let me give you the highlights of what a really good detailed market research involves.

First, you start with a Market Intelligence brief which includes:

1. Brief statement
2. Location areas & zones
3. Target market
4. Customer demographic profile

5. Cuisine
6. Venue type
7. Menu pricing
8. Competitors

Here's an example that I did for a client in Abu Dhabi, UAE, who was looking to create a new, rather large, property with multiple restaurants and bars.

For a project that size we chose to undertake an immersive deep dive into the Abu Dhabi market, looking at the existing 4 and 5-star hotels, in addition to the main independent developments, as that was where this particular operator wanted to play. When you're coming into a market that is driven predominantly by food and beverage venues in hotels, which is how the Middle East market remains to this day, gathering an understanding of the dining culture through the eyes of the independent operators gives you a great snapshot of the region and allows you to design your offering so that it is complimentary to what already exists. Remember, you are enveloping yourself in the culture of the population and the existing choices that those people have.

When doing market research, wear the hat of the operator and the hat of the guest. The data is then used to create a direction for the outlets. This piece of work can come prior or post your concept brief. If you know what you want to create, then you need to see how you can align it to the marketplace. If you have no idea what you want to do, and you're doing a snapshot of the market and going, 'What can I put in here?', this tool of generating market research is a great place to start.

CREATE TO PLATE

Interpreting the data

Let's say the reserach shows there's a gap in the market for Venezuelan cuisine. You may choose to fill that particular void. So, with this example, I am using the areas from Abu Dhabi up to and including Yas Island.

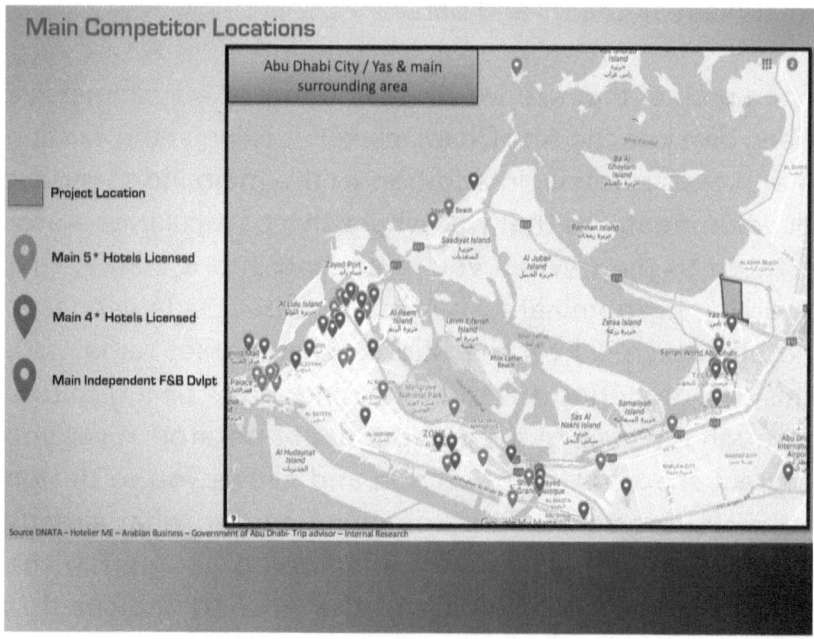

Next, you'll look at the clustering of 5-star licensed hotels and independent food and beverage developments licensed within all of those areas to see where are the pockets currently with the highest ratio of F&B market penetration. From there you divide the areas into different zones. This example shows a 30 kilometre radius from the proposed location for this property, zoned outwards from the venue. As it was 30 kilometres, you would end up with up to six zones.

THE POWER OF INSIGHT

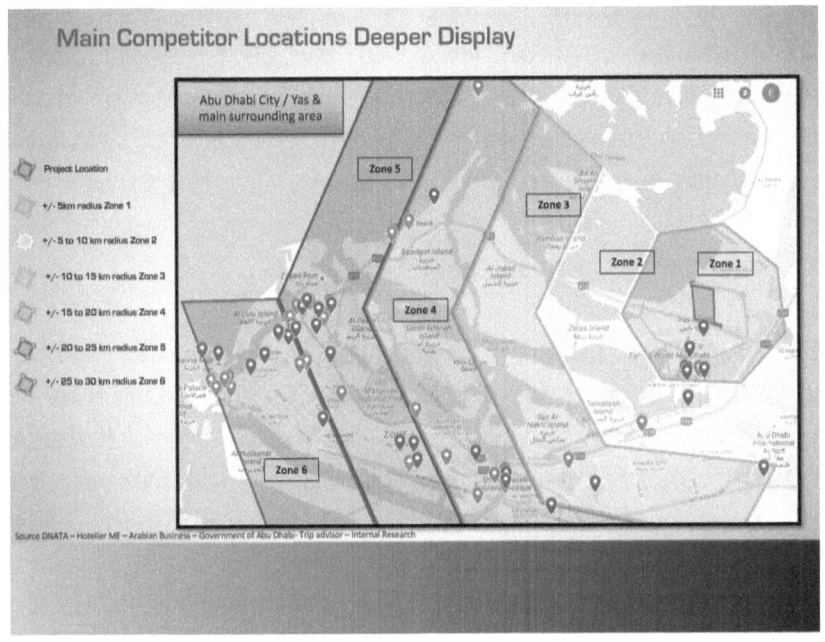

In this example we identified 180 F&B outlets, across the following generic cuisines:
- Asian
- Middle Eastern
- Italian
- International
- Bar/bar food
- French
- Latino
- Indian
- European cafe
- Sandwiches and crepes
- Seafood
- Steakhouse
- German
- Belgian
- American

CREATE TO PLATE

To break this down further, 19% of the 180 outlets were Asian in their cuisine styles, with the next highest being international and Italian, both at 10%. Following on from these were steakhouses at 7%, Middle Eastern was 5%, which was very interesting to see. By graphing that on a pie chart, we see there is obviously a massive saturation of Asian concepts in this area.

So, what does that look like from a guest's perspective? To investigate further, we want to know what awards they're getting and what's their average spend per head. If Asian was the concept that you were proposing (and I'm not saying it was at this stage) how are you going to differ from the rest of the pack?

Assess them again – are they hotel or independent? Using the example in the image above, look at zone one, which is the closest zone to where you are planning your outlet. What was the classification of these existing outlets?

Out of the 180 outlets that you found, you can then classify them into four categories: high-end, high-casual, mid-casual and casual, and there's price point differentiators across the board there. Let's say you were thinking of creating a French bistro, and you want to price it at an average spend of USD75 per head. In Abu Dhabi that was considered a high-casual environment. In that particular region, 23% of the total amount of French bistros are high-casual, while 73% are high-end. The guests are spending more than you propose to offer.

So, if you were looking to put a high-casual French bistro into this region, this snapshot gives you the insight to show that you are actually not competing with the high-end offerings.

You're actually sitting in the right market. And its only 23% of the market that's currently captured in that high-casual environment, which adds a lot of value to proceeding. The other great thing the insight gives you is a look at the density of where these operations are. Referring back to those 180 restaurants that you looked at through the zones, you are in zone one, and the density of outlets that are trading within that is only 12%. Whereas zones five and six make up about 50 to 60% of the total footprint. So you are in a very unsaturated area for your project.

You now understand that the main areas in Abu Dhabi are predominantly mid-casual price or high-casual price. In your zone (zone one) you observed a dominance in mid-casual, followed by high-casual, with the majority situated in 4 and 5-star hotels.

That gives you lots to think about!

So, the next step is to learn what the guests have to say.

Using TripAdvisor, Time Out Abu Dhabi and Google, the highest rated and reviewed outlets tended to be within the 5-star hotels and independent developments. You would be led to believe that you should focus your attention on those highly rated outlets, as they will form key competition to what you are putting forward. Another insight that you would gain is the size of the high-end market in Abu Dhabi. Keep in mind, this data is from 2016, when the market was saturated with high-end venues, and it has been in constant decline for the last few years. This is another indicator that shows the need for high and mid-casual contemporary dining experiences that provide quality and affordability at the same time. As a result of this insight, you are now able to better predict what the dining expenditure trends will likely be going forward.

Reviews also highlighted that customers were mainly complaining about lack of service and food quality within mid-casual restaurants. This insight provides you with an opportunity to change the service dynamic and offering to ensure that you focus on exceeding expectations when it comes to service and food. This operation needs to deliver a consistent experience, giving the guest a value-driven offering, and at the same time, giving the project a competitive advantage.

Ultimately, the aim is to use this insight to help produce a positioning statement based on pricing structure, offering and service deliverables.

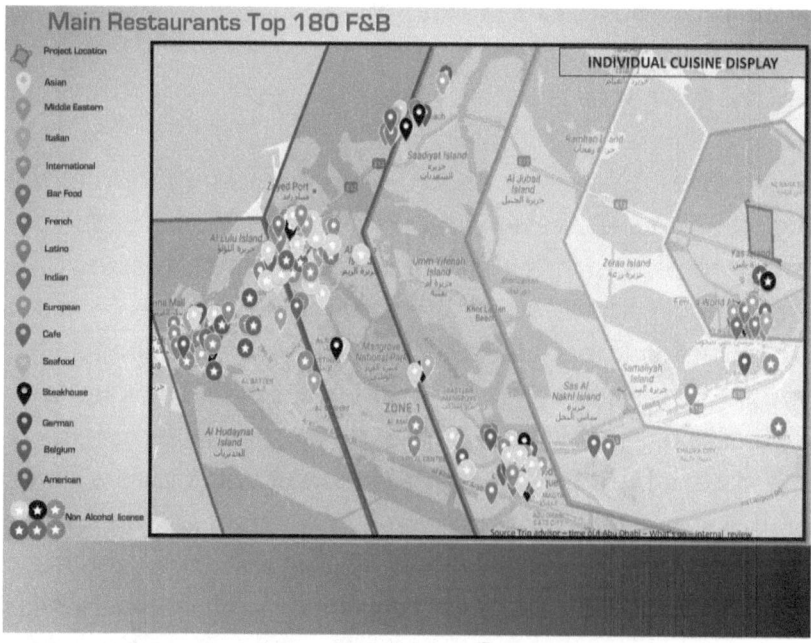

Looking at the awards for the region you quickly discovered that in zone one of your research, only 11% of total outlets were nominated, and none of them were winners! Just nominees for Time Out awards, restaurant awards, catering awards and other industry awards.

This in turn opens the potential to generate award recognition through partnering with a celebrity chef in a casual restaurant or offering a unique cooking experience, to create a dining destination with a unique point of difference. This is what was identified as lacking in the area – and from that, we know that the outlet created must offer a story with an affordable high-quality experience and soul as its foundation.

Yes, this takes time, but when you put your outlet into the market to play, which can sometimes be up to two years later, you have all of the insight to be able to ensure that what you deliver meets or exceeds the expectations of guests by enhancing the offering of what was already there.

Getting to the heart of it

There are some easier ways to do this. One of the easiest is to look at similar venues to yours and ask yourself, why do people go there? If you are creating a new Greek concept, because you like Greek food or Greek is your heritage, there will be somewhere that you've been to, that fits with your concept. That makes you think 'I like the way they do that.' Now, maybe it is, smashing the plates and that's the USP for that particular venue. So, physically go to your potential competitor and try to understand the feeling and motivation. Is it the way you are greeted? Is it the speed of service? What are the main takeaways? Then consider what will make your venue different.

Consumer insight comes from being a consumer. You are the best benchmark for what you like and don't like, and if you use that filter when creating your concept it obviously gives you a distinct advantage. I was fortunate enough to work with Michelin star chef Pierre Gagnaire on the creation of his first patisserie, cafe and lounge called Choix. It was a great opportunity because Chef Gagnaire had a particular idea of what he wanted to execute, and obviously, he knew French cuisine inside and out. But his exposure to the market where we were launching this concept (which was Dubai) was not as profound. So we undertook a significant piece of market research that involved actually going to places like Laduree, which is a Parisian concept that was exported to the Middle East. It features beautiful coffee, pastries, cakes and macarons. Actually going there gave us an insight into the elements Chef Gagnaire was looking to execute and so we took parts of that, worked and regionalised it, to the area we were in. This is a great example of market research done well, and part of the reason that Choix is still going strong today.

How you position yourself in the market leads naturally to attracting certain demographics, and a very recent example for me is our Vesper Bistro and Bar concept in Melbourne, Australia. We quickly discovered that we had two distinctly different guest profiles, which made it quite challenging to target our marketing activity. Our first guest profile was single/couples no kids, apartment living, aged 28 to 40, super mobile, high disposable income, work in all areas but specialising in freelance, from accounting through to fashion, the arts, marketing and digital. This customer profile would dine with us once or twice a month. They would dine over a long period, have cocktails, multiple courses and wine; they'd come and they'd spend big.

The other demographic was more of an established affluent group in an older age bracket, let's say, sixties plus. They dined early, came for dinner once or twice a week and ordered a main course and a glass of wine then they'd leave, not a very high average spend but they were consistent and regular. And so it was very interesting for us to look at the fact that we had these two different customer profiles, and they would all be dining in the same venue but with different motivations as to why they were there, but obviously driven by the food, beverages and atmosphere.

Whatever the ideal demographic is for your concept, whether it's fine dining or cheap and cheerful, it will be very easy to indentify through some good market research. This will work best for you based on where you are located and where you think your particular market is going to spend their money. Relaxed and subdued, versus high energy.

Now you understand that your demographics will be dictated to by the style of venue that you create, and that you may attract a different customer base from your initial thoughts as a result. Ultimately the tools for generating market and consumer insight are there to be used or not to be used. It's entirely up to you. What I wish to convey here is the value that they bring in helping you understand your potential guests before your doors are even open so that when you do open the doors, you know the demographic and the type of people who will want to walk through them.

CREATE TO PLATE

Perhaps you believe, 'If I build it, they will come' and yes, believe it or not, I've actually thought that myself in the past. But although this is a fabulous quote and I loved Kevin Costner in the movie *Field of Dreams* (1989), that's all it was – a dream. How much better to build something with the insight and understanding of what the people in your area are really looking for and then target them, cater to them. It may not be just about what you want. It actually might be about what they want. You're building hospitality venues for the consumers. Yes, part of it is for us, but at the end of the day, they need to want it.

If you are wondering, 'Can I have more than one customer profile?', I've shown by example, that of course you can, and these things may not be by choice. You may naturally find that you're attracting different customer profiles. The key here is to know in advance, who you're targeting and why.

Building up this bundle of assets to ensure you understand your target audiences allows you to tailor your messaging and your offering to attract them.

'I'm not in this for the awards,' is something I've heard many times. I'm sorry to say, but although you may not be interested in awards for being a brilliant restaurant or a popular nightclub, I can assure you that you or a member of your team will read every single review that comes out about your venue, food, and atmostphere, and positive reviews, believe it or not, are awards in themselves. Someone has actually taken the time to write a favourable review of their experience in your venue, and that is a reward and an award for you. So yes, awards are there and why not? If you've done the work, if you've put in the effort and you've created a product that your guests absolutely love, why not take the accolades? Celebrate each success!

ACTION

Visit a competitor and write down 3 things that affected you positively and 3 that were negative.
Download the Market Research template
(See RESOURCES page back of the book)

SLAM DUNK!

'Market intelligence is the sense check of your thoughts and beliefs. It provides the data necessary to back up your concept before a lease is signed and continues long after your doors are open, with every interaction you have with your guests going forward.'

CHAPTER 5

THE ART OF DESIGN

*'Earlier in my career, I needed to be the writer, casting director, set designer, leading man and producer. I've been eliminating a lot of those jobs. I'm an executive Producer right now.
I still get to pick the best screenplays.'*

Danny Meyer

The design process, from fine dining and shabby chic to deconstructed minimalistic and everything in between, impacts the way your venue looks and feels and is critical to its success. Like your concept brief, there are several key considerations that must run in parallel with this phase. Let's explore how to approach them for the best outcome in your new venue. First and foremost we need to understand the key stakeholders. This could be anyone from a kitchen designer to a landscaper to an interior designer. These key people will ensure that what you are building and creating works aesthetically as well as functionally.

Do you know why sometimes you need to sacrifice form for function? Designers are amazing individuals and I have worked with some of the best in the world. Their vision and way of interpreting your concept brief, for me in the past, has nine times out of ten blown my expectations out of the water. It is crucial to understand that they will design you something spectacular and magnificent, and they most certainly will put a lot of effort into making it look as amazing as possible. However, what you need to do here, and we'll talk about this later, is to make sure that the form does not have a negative impact on function. As beautifully designed as the place is, and I will share with you some amazing examples, if it doesn't work functionally, it just doesn't work.

You must allow it to function so that your colleagues and your employees can move freely through the venue. For example, a lot of beautifully designed, low-hanging light fittings although looking spectacular, can keep finding their way to impacting your forehead when you approach a table. This is where you need to make sure that as elegant and refined as it looks, it is still able to seamlessly function as a venue. You also need to identify where it is best to put your money and where you can save, and we will discuss what the best investment scenario is. Is it front/guest facing? Is it in the products that guests see, touch and feel, or is it in your operating equipment for your kitchen? Or a little of each?

There are ways that you can make important financial savings for yourself if you just consider changing a few things around that aren't guest facing and therefore don't need to be at the absolute highest of material specifications. How important is it to invest in and understand lighting? We will unpack a case study on lighting to uncover more on where appropriate lighting is needed. Lighting is something that really does set the mood for a venue. We don't have natural daylight 24 hours a day so it's fundamental in setting the tone and vibe of your room.

Then of course, it's also essential to understand the importance of sound and sound proofing. Sound carries – if you have a solid ceiling, solid walls and a marble floor, your sound is bounced around. Considering this in your design phase can minimise the likelihood of unneccesary financial investment in the future. Think about how you're going to reduce the impact of sound crossing over, whilst also creating an environment where people can have a conversation without having to yell.

A small tip here: when designing and space planning your venue, be sure to allow at least 10% of the super area (your entire footprint) for circulation, waiting area and washrooms. Sometimes we can forget that people have to move through the space as well as sit and enjoy it. As an example, if you've got 500 square metres of super area, allocate 50 square metres for circulation, a place for people to stand before their table is ready and to provide access into the washrooms. This has been forgotten in the past, and that's when you have chairs backing into chairs and waiters walking around with their arms above their heads just to fit through the space.

If it doesn't operate well, it will be a problem for you in the future. The quote at the beginning of this chapter is from a favourite book of mine called *Setting the Table* by Danny Meyer. It reflects that he's now got people that do the design, people that work the front of house, and he is now in a position where he gets to pick the best screenplays. And the screenplay is the canvas with which we work. And the canvas is created obviously by the designers that we work with.

The role of designers

Already, we're talking a lot about designers. So, let's now break down the role of the various designers who are involved in the creation of venues and hospitality operations.

Interior/architectural design This is the space planning for the venue and includes the floor, wall and ceiling finishes as well as overall FF&E which we have discussed during our concept briefing stage. Interior design is paramount – you will end up working very closely with this person. They will be responsible for creating the amazing look and feel you imagine for your venue, with you alongside, steering them in the right direction.

Kitchen design Yes, kitchens are designed. It is not just 'let's throw an oven in and hope for the best'! Planning for efficient kitchen operations and service flow, as well as ensuring the right equipment is selected for the task at hand is imperative. Now, a little tip here: when having your kitchen designed do not get it designed by a kitchen equipment provider. Their goal is to put as much equipment into that kitchen as possible and it will hurt your budget in the long run. If you're going to get a kitchen designer and you're not using your existing chef, get a designer that is impartial, that has no direct affiliations with equipment providers. They will design you a very efficient and effective kitchen, so that you can operate in the best possible way.

AV design Depending on the size of the venue, you may need to bring an AV design consultant in. This is ultimately the design of light and sound. It's what people see, it's what people hear and to what degree that sight and sound influences the guests' overall dining experience.

The key to good interior design is ensuring that the look and feel of the venue matches the concept brief you've created. There's nothing more important than staying true to your concept. Now, there will be a little bit of double up that occurs with your interior designer, because they will also produce mood boards or look and feel imagery. However make sure everything that you have in your original concept comes through with the designer that you're working with. Just get them to amp it up to an 11!

This brings me to one of the things I find most annoying in poor design: the size of table bases. You wouldn't believe the number of times, I've sat at a restaurant and leaned on the edge of the table and the table comes right towards me. Why? The base is too small. Yes, it looked really nice, but it doesn't work. It isn't fit for purpose.

Whether chairs have arms, through to banquettes, each must be considered both from their aesthetics as well as their function. My number one tip for selecting chairs is to get test samples and sit in the chair. If you are not comfortable in the chair, your guests will not be comfortable in the chair.

Often, these days we are getting tables and chairs custom manufactured, and that is potentially great for the look and feel of the venue, but it runs a huge risk, as you don't know how it's going to feel when you sit in it. I've had a few occasions where we've had banquette seating custom produced, and when you actually sit on it, there's not enough lower back support, it's too flat. It feels like you're sitting against a concrete wall and we've had to reject them all and get them redone.

It's super important to make sure that the tables, the chairs and the banquettes that you select with your interior designer are fit for purpose, functional, and really can give you the sense of comfort that you're looking for. If you're buying off the shelf, it's a lot easier to just go and try it. And remember, arms and no arms will forever be a great debate when it comes to chairs! I have always had a mix in all of the venues that I have done. That goes for high seating and low seating as well. Some people are just more comfortable without arms. I, for one, really like an armchair when I'm sitting down and eating, or even if I'm sitting in a club and having a few drinks. But everybody is different.

Maximising your budget and design

A few key tips on front facing furniture. If you are doing a banquette and it's covered in a fabric, a leather, alcantara or similar, the framework does not need to be a solid wood. You don't need a mahogany framework, you can use MDF. When it's not visible to the guest go with the cheaper option, especially when it comes to these sort of fittings, because then you have more money to spend on light fittings, more money to spend on artwork, more money to spend on the areas of the venue that are going to be customer facing.

THE ART OF DESIGN

If you're building and designing a beautiful bar, but have stainless steel benches all the way around stainless steel framework, that's great, but you might also be able to get away with a frame that's not stainless steel and insert the stainless steel equipment underneath it.

There are some key things to keep in mind when you're looking at where best to spend your dollars. Let's walk you through a little bit of a project here, to give you an idea of the process with an interior designer.

This example below is for a lovely rooftop lounge that we created.

We start every project by giving the design team the concept brief. They will do an interpretation of that with a look and feel presentation and a location plan of your venue. The plan is a top down view or representative layout of the location of the venue.

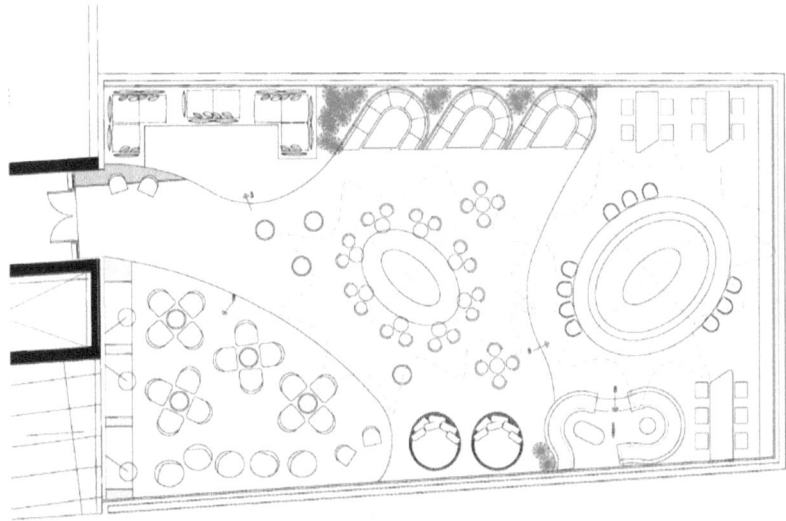

CREATE TO PLATE

Next you will see a general arrangement plan where you can identify, 'That's where my bar is. That's where my dining tables are. That's where my banquette seating is. That's where my outdoor space is. And, I've got communal seating as well!'

This is their initial layout interpretation of your concept document. It can be sketched. I have worked with sketch artists on this before, where it's done as a basic drawing that allows you to see how people move through the venue. Are the tables and chairs close enough together? Are they too close together?

It prompts you to look at how service will operate from the bar. This is the operational hat that you have on because a beautiful oval bar in the middle of a room with 30 bar stools around it may look stunning, but when someone needs to come and pick up cocktails from that point and serve to a table that is 25 feet away, you need to have a service area. Where is the service area on the bar? It's at this stage that you can work out how the space is going to function.

General arrangement plans are a great starting point, then they move on to zoning it. If you had a private dining room as part of your concept brief, then they'll zone that space. This particular rooftop had zones for a fire pit, a lower lounge area, nook seating, booth seating and a tree canopy area for general seating. Zoning allows you to see how all the areas interplay with each other and how you will service them from the kitchen or from the bar.

Inspiration is next and they will almost, every time, think of a hook or element that you didn't think about and WOW, it really does enhance the overall look of the space! For

THE ART OF DESIGN

example, in my mind, this rooftop concept originally had a very minimalistic sleek linear look to it in my concept brief. High end, sophisticated and cutting edge. When the designers looked at the space, their inspiration was more of a nautical theme. Think white ropes against blue water backdrops with massive, market umbrellas, quite a bit of cane, beautiful interwoven fabric chairs, not where I was heading at all to begin with, however, when we talked through it the purpose of it started to make sense to me that we could create this concept in a way that brought almost a Greek island feel to this venue.

The 3D renders that follow is where you actually get to see what your venue will look like when it's done. I would highly, recommend this as part of your interior design package. Get at least three renders, from three different perspectives in the venue. This is the reward for all the work and effort to this stage, with a tangible reality that you can actually look at and engage with. The 3D renders are great because they also show true perspective, and you're able to see how people will move through a venue.

CREATE TO PLATE

It also allows you to pick up things you had not yet seen. In this case, the seating that was proposed for the fire pit wrapped around the pit in the centre. In the renders, based on the space they had allocated, the pit was actually hard up against part of the seat, which we picked up through this process. We realised an area of semicircular seating couldn't be utilised because the heat of the fire pit would've made it impossible to sit there. A quick redesign resulted in a big save, as we avoided building costly seating that couldn't be used. The render is a great tool to check the functionality of the space before you build.

You can clearly see what it would be like for someone leaning up against the bar with a beer in hand and the interplay between how the guests and your colleagues is, moving through the space. Review your proposed design elements, populating your unique USP features like a water feature, a pair of macrame hammock seats suspended above a shallow pool in front of the logo. A beautiful photo opportunity and there's your Instagram moment!

That was not on my initial list of ideas, that was theirs, yet it fitted so perfectly into the venue and the type of concept that we wanted to do. The designers will propose the type of sofas, floor coverings and cushions. This is your interior designer's job, and they are there to support you to make sure that you can execute your ultimate vision.

Another quick tip here: keep them on *your* track, as they can get carried away and move you onto another path. Not intentionally but through design. Remember at all stages to stay true to your concept.

Kitchen essentials

Put on your chef's hat, quite literally, and look at how the production process in the kitchen will occur from preparation to service. Your concept brief will have stipulated whether you are looking to have a show kitchen or a back of house kitchen. Both have their proper place in designing your venue.

For those with a food offering in their venue, consideration needs to be taken as to whether you need a front facing kitchen, where the chefs can interact with your guests, or if it can remain behind the scenes. Behind closed doors is a more efficient use of space and time. The culinary direction will dictate the type of equipment you need, but I can comfortably say that there's a checklist of probably 10 to 15 items that are pretty much 90% standard across every kitchen.

Here's the essential high level kitchen considerations:

- Under bench ovens
- 6-top burner
- Refrigeration (drawer, door or walk-in cool room)
- Freezer
- Combi steamer
- Blender
- Extraction hood
- Salamandar
- Fryer
- Dishwasher

This is a basic set up that most people can execute, and of course you can add more. When we were creating a unique deli and cocktail club in Dubai, we were able to get a pork license for this venue, which is not the easiest process in the UAE. That entailed creating two kitchens in one. One kitchen produced starters, mains and desserts and one kitchen produced all of the pork elements, so that the two would not cross. We had to double up on certain pieces of equipment, but we had a competitive advantage, as we were able to serve pork products.

Even the plates, the crockery and cutlery were all different to the ones that are used for the standard kitchen so they were easily identifiable, washed and stored in a separate area. I was thankful we worked with a skilled kitchen designer, to make sure that we ticked off all of the municipality requirements.

It's important that you understand your municipality/council requirements for designing your kitchen, to make sure that you receive your certification to be able to serve food. Engaging a kitchen designer will guarantee that the kitchen is designed to your local requirements and specifications.

Light and sound in your space

How do you decide what type of lighting to use? Here is an example of where the design was wrong for the venue. It was a beautiful, dark, moody restaurant and every single individual table had a pinspot light above it. Now, for those of you that are not familiar, a pinspot is a single beam of light that perfectly covers the table top edge to edge. It looked stunning from a design perspective. You walked in and there were just these columns of light dropping down through the venue and sitting perfectly on the table, which looked great. Except our party, which was a table of six, required the restaurant to move two tables together in order to seat us, which you wouldn't think would be a problem, right? Well, because the tables were pinspotted the minute we moved one table next to the other, we lost the light on one table. It was sitting, hanging over dead air, or actually over the head of one of my guests. Operational failure.

I'm an absolute advocate of ambient and up lighting, controlled by dimmer switches so you can adjust the temperature of the lighting from warm to cool. There's nothing worse than walking into a restaurant where all the lights are on full, and it's like you're sitting in the middle of a cafeteria at your local food court. Ambience sets the tone for experience.

In parallel with this is sound. Are you going to be a music venue, a party venue, or is it a relaxed space for enjoyment? Your sound will be dictated by the type of venue that you are creating. For nightclubs, we probably need a whole separate book on the investment required for AV and your sound, lighting and projection.

As I mentioned previously, if you've got exposed floorboards and you've got hard table surfaces and hard walls and hard ceilings, you'll need to consider how to make your room suppress noise. Now this can be done in the simplest forms with carpet floor cutouts in certain sections, or you can cover the underside of your tables with sound absorbing material, similar to what you find in a recording studio.

Right now I'm working on a two-storey venue, where we have a bar and members' lounge on the ground floor and the first floor is more of an event space with a boardroom. If you are hosting a product launch in that event space and people are sitting downstairs enjoying their meal and their beverages, you don't want the sound from that event traversing either the staircase or the floor. In this instance we are using engineered sound suppressing floorboards on the first floor, which I'd highly recommend if you need a similar solution.

With all these different consultants and specialists in their fields, it looks like it can cost you a lot of money, but I cannot stress highly enough, these are things you must budget for when doing your initial planning for your venue. You will have a pot of money that you are able to spend. Your hotel owning company is going to have an allocation of money that they are going to give you to spend. Please consider these specialists now, interior design is absolutely a no brainer, but then when you've got, kitchen, lighting and sound potentially, these costs need to be factored in. Their experience is invaluable and will save you from incurring more costly rectification works in the future. Yes, you may have heated debates and discussions with your designers and they will compete to have it their way ... I've even had a very well renowned designer, actually say to me over the phone, 'It's not fair' that I had taken out part of their design. But in the end, they are there to support you to create *your* vision.

If you are sitting back now and saying, 'I just want my venue to look amazing. I don't care so much about the rest, when people walk in and they see a beautiful venue, this will really impress them!' Rest assured, you will care when the kitchen falls over on a busy Friday night, or if staff can't move between tables, when guests have their chairs slightly

THE ART OF DESIGN

out, and the doof doof music from your private dining room means guests in the restaurant can't hear themselves speak. So they may say it was a beautiful restaurant, but the waiters kept hitting the back of my chair. The food took 45 minutes to come out from the kitchen and I couldn't hear my partner talking to me because of the music from an event that was happening in a private dining room. It's absolutely worth working with professionals to master the art of design for your venue.

ACTION

Choose which of the above 3 key design elements is the most critical for you and list the 3 reasons why?
Download the sample of Design 'Look and Feel'
(See RESOURCES page back of book)

SLAM DUNK!

'It's important to listen to your designer's opinion, but always through a filter of how you can make it work operationally.'

CHAPTER 6

THE HOSPITALITY BIBLE

'Always be wary of any helpful item that weighs less than it's operating manual.'
Terry Ratt

I would love to say that the success of many of the hospitality operations over the years is down to people that just know what they are doing. While in some circumstances that actually is true, most are working with a traditional guide of standard operating procedures (SOPs) that is designed around the ethos of the concept. We need to now understand how valuable that operations bible is, not just in the initial execution, but also in the long-term sustainability of your venue.

It all starts with the re-creation of your customer journey. This is where you walk the walk of your guest. From the moment of enquiry, to the moment of departure, what are all the touchpoints that a guest has in connection with your

CREATE TO PLATE

venue? The ability to extract and record those moments is the foundation for setting up your standard operating procedures bible.

Let's talk about your systems. A 'system' is a detailed step-by-step process that is standardised and will set a consistent approach and expectation for all to follow. It can be as simple as how to answer the phone, or make an espresso, or how to plate a dish. In the past these instructions have been printed and placed in huge binders with an image and words to convey the messaging. Today I would encourage you all to create a video of each process, add it to your library of resources and make it available for your team to access online. That way, you only need to create this once saving you time constantly retraining and teaching. I can assure you your head chef will thank you if he only needs to create a video of how to plate your sea bass dish and then task his team to watch the video to learn the technique. In doing so, you will make sure that every point, from A to Z, is covered, so you can look after your guests and meet and exceed their expectations every time.

One of the great things about having a comprehensive operations bible is that it is replicable for future venues, which makes it a critical resource if you plan to export or grow your brand. In addition if you want to open a second venue in a different location, having it all documented in this way it makes life a whole lot easier.

Your operations bible will also include the information necessary to understand and implement the cleaning and maintenance requirements of your various pieces of equipment. These areas tend to get forgotten, and yet are essential to the longevity of your business and the ROI on your investment. You have invested a lot of money, especially from an equipment perspective, so it's important to establish the protocols around cleanliness and the maintenance of those areas. It is in your operations bible that you can build a schedule of maintenance and keep a record of your material safety data sheets, so that your team can make sure your equipment is always performing at the highest possible level.

Your employee manual forms a key element of the operations bible as well. These guys and girls are the cogs that make the machine work and so we want to give them all the tools that they require to be the greatest hospitality experts when they're executing their roles within your business.

Many times, new employees are thrown into the 'fire' as a 'body' on the floor with no training or induction. The problem is, 'that body' doesn't really understand your concept in that circumstance. They don't understand your service principles or how to execute them. The operations bible is the single source point that takes them on the journey from concept to your expectations, and those ultimately of your guests. No staff members should be allowed on the floor, behind the bar or in the kitchen before signing off that they have gone through this critical educational tool, ideally in video format. I cannot stress enough how important it is that they understand the concept. Even in the past, when we've had casual employees coming in for shifts on an ad hoc basis, the operations bible is something that, especially from the concept point of view, they need to understand. They're not just a body on the floor, they also need to be embedded, ingrained and indoctrinated into the concept, hence it's the keystone to ensuring consistency in execution.

A three-minute introductory video by the owner/operator on the ethos of the concepts can do this efficiently and effectively.

Traditionally, it is a big folder that will always be added to, enhanced and grown, and that's why moving it into a digital format has been something that I've found to be hugely exciting in ensuring that it's relevant to your colleagues. It would be fair to say that not having a current operations bible would be like ordering a modular shelving unit from IKEA and then throwing out the instructions before starting to build it. I know some people like this approach, but when it comes to exceptional hospitality, there's no greater thing to have than consistency (which we will cover in a later chapter).

The key things that you need to understand before diving into this section in creating your operations bible are:

- your concept as detailed in your Concept Brief
- the customer journey (which forms the basis of your systems for sequence of service and your business operations)
- the employee manual (the step-by-step systems to get your team on board, engaged and operating)
- the equipment inventory, as well as a cleaning and maintenance schedule

Creating your operations bible

It's very important that the first step you take in creating your operations bible is to walk in the shoes of your guests. This will give you the pinch points of service to meet and exceed guest expectations and help to build your sequence of service from the ground up.

No two operations bibles are the same. There are no two businesses that operate exactly the same, unless you're working in a franchised or licensed environment. To help you pull it together, I will show you how to build an operations bible step by step, using the example of the creation of the world's first 'MasterChef, the TV Experience' restaurant.

This was the realisation of my long held goal and vision, to create an environment where guests had the opportunity to taste and experience food that was created on the global television phenomenon that is MasterChef.

For those of you unfamiliar with the TV show, it is an internationally recognised and award-winning reality cooking show with contestants competing in cooking challenges set by the judges and guest celebrity chefs, created and televised in over 200 territories to over 300 million people. I'd had this idea for quite a few years before we were able to actually materialise it.

I needed to build the concept from scratch and work with the parent company in the UK, Banijay Group (formerly Endemol Shine), in order to make sure that we created an experience for the restaurant guests that enhanced or augmented their expectations based on what they had seen on the TV show.

The way we did that was by immersing ourselves in the brand and then creating a way to immerse the guests in the brand. It's an example of taking a concept that is not designed to be a restaurant and turning it into a restaurant.

CREATE TO PLATE

Fortunately for me, the heart and soul of the restaurant was pretty much dictated by the nuances of the MasterChef contestants and champions who contributed their vision and recipes and the driving force behind them. The question was how to re-create those dishes in a restaurant environment to ensure that we maintained that same level of execution, to the same level of standards that won these champions their competitions?

This was the biggest operations bible I've ever created simply because it had not been done before, and we were taking food from a television show and re-creating it in a restaurant environment in a much shorter window.

For those of you that have seen the show, some of these dishes can take up to three hours to prepare, and no guest is willing to sit in a restaurant and wait three hours for their main course! So, we needed to come up with a way, a system and a sequence by which we could, execute all of these dishes, within a realistic timeframe, while still giving the guests the MasterChef USP that differentiates the outlet from others. Taking the ordinary and making it extraordinary!

The build of the operations bible started with identifying the six key elements that would ultimately contribute to the whole picture of how we would execute MasterChef, the TV Experience.

Fortunately, we had brand guidelines and logos that had been created, however we needed to make sure that every time the name was mentioned, every time the logo was used, the colour palette that we used, all this was in keeping with the established brand. There were specific details for all communications that ensured every piece of marketing collateral that went out, every social media post that went out, how we needed to talk about the brand, what words we could use, were all on brand.

When referring to the restaurant concept, it was always quoted as 'MasterChef, the TV Experience'. From this, we learned quite quickly the fences we were bound by with the original brand. Now it was time to take that and create our own.

The development of the style guide gave us our parameters to work in. Obviously, we then made sure that anything we did was also acceptable to the brand guardians. We had a very specific framework to play within.

Bringing together your team

We needed to work out how many people were required to operate the venue effectively. The idea behind it all was to create a MasterChef experience, but it wasn't just based on one region's programming – no, we wanted to utilise the TV programs from across the globe and intermingle the dishes into one cohesive menu. Dishes from MasterChef champions such as Simon Wood from the UK, Shaun O'Neale from the USA, Elena Duggan and Diana Chan from Australia, to name a few.

We needed the right people in the kitchen to be able to re-create those amazing recipies. Getting your staffing needs established early is critical. From there you can flesh out the job descriptions. For this venue, we had 12 unique job descriptions just for back of house.

CREATE TO PLATE

When it came to front of house, we knew we needed to hire big personalities that could understand and explain each dish, who created it and why. There was always a story behind each dish that ended up being on the inaugural menu and those stories were amazing. Some of them, were inspired by their grandmother's cooking, when they went to their country farmhouse as a child, and they remembered the senses and the flavours. We put all of those individual experiences and information into the operations bible for reference.

New staff onboarding took a significant amount of time because we had to make sure that when a guest asked a question, they had an answer. The brand and concept was too important for us not to take the time to do that in the most minute detail. We ended up with 16 individual job descriptions for front of house

Now we move onto our operating systems. This covers everything from how to set a table to how to fillet a fish – each individual procedure that you need to have undertaken should be recorded on video and documented. This is broken down into sections that include kitchen recipes, a restaurant checklist, your opening procedures, your closing procedures, your cleaning procedures, your cashing up procedures – all of that sits under your operating systems and they are specific to each venue.

So if you're doing a Turkish restaurant, and you've got live music in the venue, there might be periods of time when service is not as present on the floor while the music is playing and a whirling Dirvish is performing. You would not want service walking through the Dirvishes' routine. There would need to be a system in place to ensure consistency.

The next element is all of your training programs, for your beverages, your front of house training lists, any handouts that you create, any presentations that you've done, all of this needs to sit in a training folder in the operations bible that your colleagues can access. Again make it all video based and online so it is always available for future hires to see.

Your whole team has access to the bible, and for new hires and new starters, it's *the* training tool. It's a learning tool for them to get up to speed with the way things are done in the venue, and to get a handle on all of your menus and all of your recipes.

Recording your dishes

From a back of house perspective, make sure that all your previous and current menus are there: your beverage menus, your event menus and set menus.

We had a unique selling point at MasterChef, the TV experience: 'The Mystery Box'.

The mystery box challenge on the TV show is where the judges present the contestants with a box of ingredients. The contestants then have a limited amount of time to produce a dish utilising, some, or all, of those ingredients depending on the challenge. I took that and turned it a little bit on its head. I wanted to have a mystery box where, the guest chooses a set number of the ingredients in the box and then our chefs have 45 minutes to produce and serve an amazing dish. I chose 45 minutes specifically, as being a relevant time it should take to place an order and for a main course to be served. On completion, the chef would produce a handwritten recipe of the unique dish, and give it to the guest so they could take it home and replicate it. We had some truly inspirational outcomes with these boxes and the guests thoroughly enjoyed this particular aspect of the *EATertainment* experience.

Initially, our head chef was the only person who could execute this challenge. So every time we did a mystery box in the early days, we wrote the recipes down, recorded their execution and put them in the operations bible, so that we could train up the sous chefs and chef de parties to learn how to approach these mystery boxes. We designed pre-thought out approaches to make sure that we could deliver something of extraordinary quality and that the guests would find memorable.

Next we included an image library of photos or videos of dishes, anything that's gone up on social media, group photos, team photos, again, these are things that you can use going forward to celebrate the successes, and the execution of your concept.

If you ever do consider going down the path of franchising or licensing your venue, having a package of imagery and video content with established systems to give to a designer, makes the design phase and that process a whole lot easier to execute. One of the key things with the operations bible is that even though front of house and back of house are technically separate entities, these days I refer to them as the *heart of house*. The operations bible is really a guide for your heart of house team.

Equipment inventory

When it comes to equipment, an accurate up to date inventory of all of your operating equipment, along with the cleaning procedures and regular maintenance is a living document within your operations bible. Equipment represents a significant portion of the investment outlay in the creation of your venue. Whether you are buying into an existing business or building a business from the start, it is hugely important that the assets that you purchase are looked after. They're expensive initial purchases and require regular attention much like any long-term relationship.

The operations bible keeps a listing of how to take care of those expensive pieces of equipment that you have. You might have a 'Slayer' coffee machine – they can run into the tens of thousands of dollars. You need to know how to maintain that coffee machine properly. It's not just one person's responsibility. Someone who may never have managed it before needs to have access to a document or video that tells/shows them how to clean the machine at the end of a service. Make sure this is all available in the operations bible to support the longevity of your business.

Move your operations bible online, get it all into Dropbox or another cloud-based storage facility. That way, people can tap into it from their phones, from their tablets, from their laptops. In this day and age it doesn't need to be a physical binder that's gathering dust on a shelf somewhere. I know, 'OMG, more work, more work!' Yes. This is one area where you put the work in now to reap the benefits on the day you open the door.

CREATE TO PLATE

You may be saying, 'It's a lot of pre-work, can't the team just figure it out as they go?' I'm sure some of them can, but they're also going to bring their own ideas from what they've experienced previously. They may have worked under a business with its own operations bible that still relys on paper-based SOPs, that might run contrary to the way you want to run your business. This is where we must remove any inconsistencies in delivery – and more than that, any opinions. You set the tone, you set the standard, and between yourself and your operations team, you will build the SOPs for the business. Collectively, you might have 10 people working for you, and they've all worked at 10 different businesses. Now, each one of those businesses may have some policies and procedures that absolutely fit in with what you're doing, but what you're doing is bringing them into your way of working. Not the other way around.

We would all wish our entire team had exactly the same passion as we do for our business but it's not always the case. We need to rely on our systems to execute on a consistent, unified basis. If you have an operations manager or a restaurant manager you can allocate out certain tasks in building the operations bible. They will have worked on these things before. But it's crucial that the operations bible sets the tone. It really creates the environment for your team to understand what it is that you want to achieve and provides all the tools for them to be able to deliver it.

It does seem like a lot of work for something that will likely just sit on a shelf or in the background for years to come. But that's the past. We've all had times where we've picked up the ops bible and blown three and a half years of dust off it. However, these days it's a living cloud-based entity that is constantly being enhanced and updated. It should reflect the perfect snapshot of your venue in that moment, where current licenses and certificates are all available. In this day and age, it has to be digital. So, if you put the work in at this stage, before your first guests walk through the door, when they do arrive, and they will, you and your team can focus on the first-class delivery and execution of your vision.

ACTION

Write down 5 experiences you have had as a customer/guest that have left a memorable impression on you.
Use those as the basis to set up your first systems (stealing with pride).

SLAM DUNK!

'Technology is great. Put the entire operations bible in Dropbox or any other third-party cloud provider. Give access to each one of your team, then use DocuSign to get them to sign at the end to show that they have read it.'

CHAPTER 7

PASSION VS. PROFIT

'Basically the best financial models are simple enough for anyone to understand yet dynamic enough to handle complex situations.'

Tim Vipond

We can't do any of this without money, both invested and then ultimately received. I'd love to say that we could manifest hospitality venues without an investment, but that just doesn't happen.

So let's now look closely at the financial factors you need to consider to ensure you don't overcapitalise your investment:

- Key assumptions
- Weekly profile
- Payroll assumptions
- Pre-opening expenses

CREATE TO PLATE

Understanding these elements will allow you to set realistic, optimistic monetary goals and targets for your performance once you open.

In this chapter, we'll take a step-by-step approach to understanding everything from assumed fit-out cost to rolling year budget, to get a good overall indication of how much we need to invest and how much we can expect to see return. Not everyone loves numbers, but remember, you can't have romance without finance! Just for now, we need to take the emotion out of our vision and approach our concept from a financial point of view. Yes, it does take a little bit of the heart out of everything you've done up to this point – but this is the time to focus on where to best put your money and not let the emotion of all of the wonderful things that you're creating get ahead of you.

I'll start by saying, you need to be honest about your numbers – and you must always be ready to adjust your programming and assumptions based on the results of the modelling.

Here's a quick example. To begin with, you might think that the average spend in your restaurant will be $200 a head. But when you start to break it down and put up some of the dishes that your new chef has created, you might find out that it's only $125 a head. If things change, you must be ready to swiftly adapt, because the numbers won't be real otherwise. When you push those numbers back into your model, you'll start to see where your investment is sitting. You can then start to understand exactly when your ROI is becoming realistic.

It's also important to understand from the start that increased budgeted revenue does not necessarily mean more profit. I am being controversial here, but many times I have presented a budget or a financial model for a business where the owners come back to me and say, 'It's not showing enough revenue, increase the revenue up by 20%!' And I have to sit there and have the debate and say, 'I can show that, but then we're not looking at real numbers.'

It's so critical to be realistic with your modelling and forecasting. Unrealistic assumptions have the potential to lead to real financial challenges when you open your venue. One of the worst things you can do is forget to include ramp-up stages. I tend to use six months as a good ramp-up number. As an example, let's say that, over 12 months, I want to make a million dollars in revenue. And so, I just divide a million dollars by 12 months, right? Wrong! That's not accurate financial modelling. Instead, what you need to work out is, if I'm ramping-up in the first six months, what will I make as I build the business up? As an example, I might project $50k in month one, $60k in month two, $65k in month three, $75k in month four, $89k in month five and $92k in month six.

In this case, how much do I then need to make from month seven to month 12 in order to hit my million dollar annual target? That is how you need to approach modelling. (FYI – it would be $95k per month for the rest of the year).

Understanding the monthly trends in your location is also important. For example, do school holidays affect your business? Does the weather affect your business? Are you in a ski field where you only trade six months of the year?

What's more, simply thinking, 'I want to make a million dollars in revenue this year' is not giving you the full picture. You also need to work out how much you need to allocate to your costs (often 90%) and then work with what is left as your profit (often 10%). In other words, you will need to sell 'x' amount in order to make 'x' amount in order to have 'x' amount to pay for your costs. Then, what you have left is your true profit.

Right now, in the early stages when you have an idea, your modelling can literally start on the back of a napkin. However, when you're looking to actually make an investment, you'll need a more precise tool. So for now, do the paper napkin test, to make sure that your idea is viable. Then use a modelling tool to make sure that what you expect to make is what you can genuinely return.

The hospitality industry is a complex, dynamic field. We have a lot of different areas where when costs blow out in one area, it can impact another and this automatically impacts your profitability. Financial modelling allows you to look at all of your costs going in before you put any significant money in at all. Modelling allows you to see that if your food cost goes up by 5%, what impact that will have on your profitability. If your restaurant general manager wants $10,000 more a year than what you're prepared to offer, how might that affect your profitability? You can learn all this using modelling, without having to actually test it in real time with real money.

Imagine putting your life savings into something that you love based purely on a hunch that it will work out. Your chances of success are slim (at best). Without a clear understanding of your financial position, they are next to none. So, let's walk though the key financials you need to understand before you start.

We'll start by defining and establishing your key assumptions. These are your direct inputs on the space that you're taking, such as the overall size (inside and out), amount of rent to be paid, cost of insurances, monthly outgoings year on year, revenue growth assumptions, all of that. From there, you can build your weekly profile. This is the high-level snapshot of your expected number of guests spread across food and beverage assumptions based on your concept. You also have your payroll assumptions, which are obviously capturing your labour costs plus on-costs (never forget the on-costs) and your pre-operating expenses, which are the costs associated with company set up, licensing, training, food trials, website, marketing and more. You will then build in a basis of operating capital, which is that six month phased growth period that I talked about before, which allows you to fund your venue until you reach the time where you are breaking even or making money.

If this is sounding confusing, stick with me. There is also an opportunity at the back of the book to receive a template for a financial model to help you on your journey.

Key assumptions

As mentioned above, the key assumptions are our base, our starting point. What are the costs we need to put into the development of this hospitality venture? What's the functional currency that we're dealing in? This allows the model to be used across different countries. I've set mine up to work in US Dollars, Emirati Dirham, British Pounds and Australian Dollars.

What space are we playing in? This is the super area I have referred to previously. Let's start with how much internal and external space we have. In this example, we'll call the venue Chez Fraser, and I'm saying we've got 140 square metres of internal space and a 20-square metre terrace. What is the fit-out cost per square metre or capital spending? This is an assumption on the investment per square metre required to create your venue. This can slide up and down from economy to luxury, but as a good rule of thumb, I use a benchmark of around USD1300 per square metre. If you're working in square feet, 10.76 square feet equals one square metre.

Now, put in an allocation for pre-opening marketing. We will talk about the launch of the venue later in the book but a good assumption would be 2–3% of your fitout cost. The model is fluid and these numbers can scale up or down as well.

We then put in some fixed expenses. If you're committed to a lease for a venue (this is for the owner-operators right now) you populate your rent per square metre. Don't forget to factor in a rental increase per year. If you were to do a financial model over five years, your rent is not going to stay the same. So, include a year over year percentage increase, somewhere between 3–5%.

Once you've got your business through its ramp-up phase into what we call stabilisation, where it's consistently trading at a certain level, what do you assume your year on year growth will be, after two years? Then, subsequently, what are your cost of sales as a percentage of revenue? The general rule for those of you just jumping in for the first time, is to assume 25–35%, depending on where you work.

Outlet overheads is a percentage of revenue. Again, this is a figure that's estimated, but generally somewhere between 15–17% is a good summation. I also then allocate in some fees because we will dealing with third party companies, so this may include technical fees, marketing fees, a PR agency on a retainer, etc. That's your hard data.

Please provide the following key data (fill in all yellow cells)

	Data		Comments	Explanations/Notes
Outlet Name	Chez Fraser		Project/Outlet name (in words)	
Functional Currency	AUD		Being operating currency (e.g. USD/AED/BHD/GBP)	
Area				
Internal Area		140	In square meters	
Terrace Area 1		20	In square meters (if applicable, otherwise leave blank)	
Terrace Area 2			In square meters (if applicable, otherwise leave blank)	
Capital Spending				
Fit out cost/square meter		1,800	Capital cost/square meter or total spend divided by square meters. If working in square feet then 10.76 square feet = 1 square meter	
Marketing - Pre-opening		5000	The anticipated investment in marketing pre-opening	
Rent				
Rate/square meter		750	If working in square feet then 10.76 square feet = 1 square meter, please adjust accordingly to rate per square meter	
Rent increase year on year		3%	Assumed rate of rental increases year on year, for example 5%	
Growth rates				
Year on year revenue growth		5%	% growth rate of revenues after 2 year ramp up	
Other cost assumptions				
Cost of sales % of revenue		30%	Assumed cost of sales % based on gross revenue	
Outlet overheads as % of revenue		15%	Assumed other overheads as % of revenue	Excluding GST

Fee Data			
Fee Summary			
Initial Fee		_____	in operating currency
Technical Fee		0%	in operating currency
Continuing Fee		_____	as %
Marketing Fee		5%	as %

Weekly profile

We'll now look at what you are producing, which is the Weekly Profile. What is your weekly average cover profile?

CREATE TO PLATE

In other words, the number of covers per sitting? This input depends on your trading days and meal periods, like breakfast, lunch, brunch and dinner, and whether you offer takeaway or delivery.

Your weekly profile is where you capture all of that data. Here's an example of a business that trades six days a week. The profile assumes that on a Tuesday, Wednesday and Thursday, it will do on average of 32 covers for lunch. Then, on a Friday and Saturday it will do 40 and on a Sunday it will do 60 for brunch. If we capture that Tuesday lunch element and assume 25 covers for lunch, what do we believe they will spend per person on food? What do we believe they will spend per person on beverages?

If you assume, based on your concept, that each guest will spend an average of $45 on food and $20 for beverages, that gives you a total average of $65. While you still can not see whether that's a realistic number or not, it does allow you to start to build a model to see your potential daily revenue. You can also capture similar assumptions around takeaway and delivery if that is something you want to offer.

PASSION VS. PROFIT

Please provide the following key data (fill in all yellow cells)

Business Forecast Data

Weekly Average Cover Profile - number of covers per sitting

	Monday	Tuesday	Wednesday	Thursday	Friday	Saturday	Sunday	Average Food Cheque	Average Beverage Cheque	Average Total Cheque
Breakfast								0		0
Lunch		25	35	35	40	40		45	20	65
Brunch							60	80	40	120
Dinner	40	40	40	60	60	65		85	40	125
Other (specify)										0
Other (specify)										0
Totals	40	65	75	95	100	105	60			

Take out/delivery average number of deliveries/takeouts - number of orders

	Monday	Tuesday	Wednesday	Thursday	Friday	Saturday	Sunday	Average Food Order	Average Beverage Order
Take out lunch									0
Take out dinner									0
Delivery lunch									0
Delivery Dinner									0
Totals	0	0	0	0	0	0	0		

	Weekly
Breakfast per week	0
Lunch per week	175
Brunch	60
Dinner	305
total	540

Payroll assumptions

This is one of the highest costs that you'll be dealing with once you've completed your venue. Make sure you position yourself correctly in the market for what it is you're offering, depending on the style of venue and the responsibilities of the different people. You have already carved out those responsibilities in your operations bible and the job descriptions that you created, so you now need to provide a salary that is representative and commensurate with the role that you're asking them to do. You may be governed by labour laws and agreed wage rates in your area, so be sure to check that first before populating.

Remember, this is not about being stingy. Your 'heart of house' are the ones who will actually make you money and you need to invest in them in order to create. Using a restaurant example, you will most likely have a restaurant manager, an assistant restaurant manager, supervisors, floor staff and you might have a reception area with receptionists and hostesses along with service staff, captains and runners. And then back of house, you'll have your head chef, sous chef, chef de parties, demi chefs, apprentices and kitchen porters.

Don't forget to add your total related costs, things like housing allowances, health insurance cover, gratuity and the like. We usually calculate this by a multiplication factor, for instance, in Australia, the allocation of superannuation benefits is 10% of the total base salary. With payroll now factored in, you get to see if your revenue assumptions subtracted by your payroll assumptions will give you a profitable outcome.

Pre-operating expenses

The next tier in the modelling is your pre-opening expenses. This includes things that don't get considered in financial assumptions such as recruitment fees or training. You may need to use a recruitment agency, especially to hire some of your key staff, and it's likely that once you find the right people, they're not all going to arrive on day one. Keep in mind, you will need to have them on board probably two to three weeks in advance to train them up and get them ready.

Another pre-operating cost to factor in is that of setting up your company. The amount varies across different regions, but there will be fees of some description. So, whether you're registering as an LLC or you're registering as a Pty Ltd, there will be a cost associated that you'll need to cover.

If an online presence is important to you (and I would say for all of you, it's critically important), the potential to generate business through your website is immense. So, be sure to also include a cost for creating your website, along with other essential marketing collateral, such as business cards and menus.

What about any compliance that you need to adhere to? For example, do you need food handling certificates? Do you need to provide them for your team or are they obtained by the team independently? Do you need certification licensing or a food authority certificate to be able to serve food? Do all of your staff need to have undertaken a responsible service of alcohol course in order to be able to serve alcoholic beverages?

Don't forget health and hygiene too – if there's training that needs to happen, schedule it in and budget for it.

Food trials and soft openings is something that is often forgotten about when modelling and budgeting, but this is an essential step in the pre-opening of your restaurant. You will be spending money on food and getting no revenue for it, so make sure you factor an amount to cover off the cost of providing that food, so that when you do open the door to paying customers, the recipes have been tried and tested. Allocate for small wares too, which are always forgotten when focusing on the bigger picture.

CREATE TO PLATE

Economic Model for Chez Fraser					
Super Area in Sq. Mtrs. (Covered) - TBC			140	Terms as per proposal	Area in Sq Mtrs.
Terrace -TBC			20	Covered area	140
Super Area in Sq. Ft.			1,722	Terrace	20
BOH area at 30% of total area (assumption)			(603)	Total Area	160
Area for aisles, waiting area, washrooms at 10% of super area			(172)		
Capacity			947		
Area for number of seat at 14 sq. ft. per seat of FOH space			67.63		
Revenue per day in functional currency			5,685		

Financials	Forecasted financials (YR 1)		Forecasted financials (YR 2)	
		AUD		AUD
Annual Revenue		2,074,976		2,603,627
Labour cost - incl superannuation	-34%	(712,845)	-29%	(748,487)
Cost of sales	-30%	(622,493)	-30%	(781,088)
Advertising and Marketing - Central contribution	-5%	(103,749)	-5%	(130,181)
Restaurant overheads	-15%	(311,246)	-15%	(390,544)
Rent	-4%	(83,020)	-4%	(108,171)
Other	0%	-	0%	-
Other	0%	-	0%	-
EBITDA		241,623		445,156

	Revised		
Total Capital outlay			
	Rate per sq. ft.		AUD
Super Area	1,722	168	288,536
Pre-Ops			
Recruitment fee/ Month		-	
Training/ Month		20,000	
IT Infrastructure		10,000	
Company Set up		2,000	
Pre-opening Marketing		5,000	
Technical Fee		5,000	
RSA Compliance		2,000	
Website & Colateral		10,000	
Health & Hygiene		2,000	
Food trial and soft opening		2,000	
Small wares		1,000	
Total pre-ops		59,000	
Contingency			28,853.63
Total Capex			376,390
Payback period in Years / months - * refer Details working		0.74	*

The financial model

By combining our key assumptions, weekly profile, payroll assumptions and our pre-opening expenses, we get a snapshot of the viability of the business. An economic model. So, does the model make sense? As you can see from the image, the economic summary gives us basically our super area in square metres, including any terrace area or outside areas, uncovered areas, etc, then it allocates an area for back of house. We tend to use 30% of the total area as a starting point. It's an assumption, but in general, 30% of your total footprint should be allocated to back of house. Then we allocate 10% of the super area for aisles, waiting areas and washrooms, which I have mentioned previously.

That then gives us an estimate of the seating capacity we actually have. We calculate the seat per person by allocating 14 square feet per individual to fill that space. To explain that calculation, let's say that you've got 1000 square feet of space – if you allocate 14 square feet per person, it gives you a seating capacity for roughly 72 guests. This is great input for planning, and is really valuable when setting up your venue.

The model gives you a high-level snapshot of how much revenue you have, all the costs that are associated with it, and if its profitable? Done? Yes, if there is profit and no if there isn't. That's when you've got to go back to your assumptions model and think, right, how do I make this work?

When revising your model, it's not just about changing your revenue. As I stipulated previously, it's about looking at other areas within your business to manage your cost structure. You haven't opened your doors yet and you already have an idea as to whether it's a profitable venture or not. You might see your capital expenditure as $400,000. You might see your profitability as $200,000 in year one and $250,000 in year two. You know then (roughly) that for your $400,000 investment, you're going to get your money back in around a year and seven months.

This is also a great time to have a look at how you plan to invest and where you are investing your money. You might find that your overall capital expenditure is way above what your profitability repayment is going to be to generate your ROI. In another example, I was late onboarding to a project in Dubai with Michelin star chef Greg Malouf, and we inherited a lot of the design for the venue. By this time, it was challenging to change it. The great thing about the venue was that it was a massive space –18,000 square feet!. Using the financial modelling, we were able to create an amazing kitchen for Greg to work in, given that we had so much space. The front of house was beautifully designed, including metres and metres of leather floor tiles.

Now, leather floor tiles look absolutely stunning. They look amazing, but they do not have a good durability factor. And so if it had been a huge venue with lots of spaced out seating and people were coming in for three hour Michelin-style dinners, yes, I could see that potentially those floor tiles would have worked. But, our opening night had 800 people jumping up and down to a DJ playing deep house (Paris Hilton!) ... and yes, you guessed it, those floor tiles didn't last. Not past night one! This was one of those things that we could have value engineered out at an earlier stage when it wouldn't have cost as much money to do, and we would've had a lot more longevity out of the flooring.

The modelling gives you the chance to look at your numbers, in reality. It gives you the data you need to help you look at individual areas and decide if that is where you want to spend your money. It also helps you identify potential areas where you can save your money. It is here that you can actually value engineer some things in order to make them more reliable and durable. Yes, they might look great, but ultimately are they going to serve their purpose? Your financial model gives you a great way to look at that. On top of this, if you look like you're overcapitalising on your venue or over-investing, then you get to stop at this moment and say right, hold everything. Let's look back at it all again, because these numbers are not working.

Just one final point on these inputs – they are great to then put through your financial model for your net present value (NPV) or your internal rate of return (IRR). Net present value is simply the value of cash inflows and the present value of cash outflows over a period of time. The internal rate of return is a calculation used to estimate the profitability of a potential investment. So by factoring all of this in, you get a very good overview of the sustainability and the wellbeing of your proposed business.

The really good thing about this is, you may not necessarily know how much you're going to spend at this point in time, so this modelling tool will give you an indication of what it's going to cost you. This allows you to either step back and say, 'Oh no, that's too expensive for me. I'm not going to invest in that at this point in time.' Or you might think, 'Oh, I'm underinvesting I actually want to spend more.' The money you want to invest is shown as a projection of when it comes back which also gives you an opportunity to look at your potential payback. This allows you to have more control over the money that you are investing.

Some will say, 'I'll just leave it up to the accountants.' I would challenge that by saying they will definitely play a part in this, but at the end of the day, it's your money. Don't you want to know where it's going, and how much you can potentially make?

CREATE TO PLATE

I think that the people who don't get involved at this stage and in these elements miss out on a huge opportunity to save more and to potentially generate more. I have worked with operators that say, 'Well, if my costs are too high when we open, I'll just cut staff and get cheaper products in.' I say, then we may as well not even be here because that is basically killing off the identity and the DNA of the concept that you have spent all this time creating!

Remember the modelling process is used to give you an idea of your overall financial position before you invest a dollar. Wouldn't you feel better making minor adjustments and tweaks along the way and still keep the authenticity of the concept well and truly alive?

We haven't really talked about money until this time in the book because it does clash with the creativity side. However, as I said before, you can't have romance without finance. The romantic period is the courtship stage, which has gotten us to this point – now we have to fund it.

ACTION

Fill out the table with your Weekly Profile assumptions and get a snapshot of your weekly proposed sales. *(See RESOURCES page back of book)*

SLAM DUNK!

'Modelling can start on the back of a napkin. Some of the best and most successful entrepreneurs that I know and have worked with, started right there, with very quick, very big, high-level numbers.'

CHAPTER 8

HIRE BETTER THAN YOU

'Service comes from a manual. Hospitality comes from the heart.'

Kirk Kinsell

I've always strived to open venues that have a lived-in feeling about them. Yes, you can achieve a lot of that through the design, but ultimately it's the people that bring the heart, warmth and soul to your venue. What we're looking at in this chapter is, how do we hire better than ourselves *(Hire Higher!)*? What are some of the steps we can take to ensure that we get the right people into the business? We'll also break down the importance of personality over skill.

A massive shift has occurred in recruitment in hospitality over the last 10 to 15 years. Before then, everything was about achievement, experience and how many degrees you have. Today, yes, give me an example of your experience, that's definitely one part of it, but we also need to understand the importance of personality. Hospitality is showbusiness, we're in the entertainment industry and we need personalities to engage with.

You will also learn why every person you have in their role must be better at that one singular job than you. We've only touched on egos briefly in the book, but I'm sure you can guess why hiring a team of professionals that are better at their job than you are is a really smart move.

We will then expose you to the two key rules of engagement. Firstly, always hire slowly, take your time, don't rush and don't over-promote. And secondly, you need to be able to fire quickly. It's hard I know, and it's not an easy topic to discuss, but it's for the betterment of your business. Ultimately, no matter how good your food or beverage offering is or how great the space looks and feels, your team are 100% responsible for you either making money or losing it.

Personnel is the most important aspect of hospitality operations. It's one of the areas that we spend the most amount of money on and it's vital that the people we bring in are there to benefit the overall concept. They're an integral part of your day-to-day operations. Everyone can be taught something, but personality is not something you can teach. So I always hire on personality and if there are gaps in the skills areas, then I'm happy to train them.

Looking through the lens of not investing the time to hire and recruit the right team, places all of your other assets at risk of either being underutilised or not utilised at all. Set yourself up for success by hiring who you want, not what you need.

So what do we mean when we talk about personality? It's that first impression that you get, when someone's inner soul shines through. It's that feeling of warmth, the part that makes you laugh or cry.

Why do they need to be better at the job than you are? Well, as operators we need to be a jack of all trades. However, when hiring your key positions, it's imperative that your people are better than you at the job that they're given. A quick example would be, if I'm looking to hire a mixologist, I'd want them to make better cocktails than I do. I know how to make a Negroni, but I want someone that I'm hiring to do it better than me.

Finding personalities that shine

When building a conceptual hospitality brand, and identifying the type of personalities that you want to have in your venue, you must look at different ways of recruiting, different ways of getting people to come on board.

So the example I'm sharing with you here is with MasterChef, the TV Experience again. The personalities were crucial to the execution of this brand and to bring that concept to life. Some of you may have experienced open recruitment days where applicants come in with their CVs and sit down with you for an often very quick, brief interview. There are lots of people coming in and out. It's all kind of mismatched and unstructured.

Well, we wanted to approach it quite differently. We wanted to have people come in that were already engaged, already understood the concept from a high level and could sell us on their understanding and suitability for the role. To start, we invited all of our senior roles, from assistant managers to sous chefs, to submit a two-minute video telling us why they wanted to come and work with us.

We'd given them an understanding of what the concept ideation was and then they needed to talk to us about how they were going to bring their personality, skills and talent to augment that concept. As a litmus test we knew that if someone said, 'Oh, I don't really want to send a video in of myself' then they were probably not the sort of outgoing, gregarious individuals that we were looking for. This process also allowed us to audit the applications much more quickly at this early stage.

To their credit, some people submitted very creative video productions, utilising different settings and locations and cutting from one scene to another. And importantly, showing us they understood what the television show was all about.

Once we had finalised and collated all of these 'video finalists' we invited them all to an open audition day. We put some time into this and created four different tests/experiences, depending on the job functionality. It was one day only, so where you invest your recruitment dollars is obviously critical.

You might put ads up on a website, use a talent agent or recruiter. We decided to throw all our eggs into one basket and took over a test kitchen. Obviously our venue wasn't completed, but this test kitchen had multiple cooking stations and a mock-up event space. We didn't tell anyone what they were doing in advance of the day. We just told them that they were to turn up at a certain time. Shuttle buses were organised to pick them up from a centralised location and to bring them over to the venue, making it as easy as possible for them and to remove any barriers to their attending the day. Once they arrived, they discovered that they were about to undertake several tasks.

The chefs would arrive with an apron and their knives. They were greeted by the head chef, who tasked them with doing a mystery box. They had no idea what the ingredients were underneath the box and they were given an hour to prepare one dish, either sweet or savoury.

Once their dish was completed, the head chef, myself and the restaurant general manager tasted them all and made our own notes as to who would recieve an offer letter the following day. We were able to see their cooking skills in a manufactured but still stressful environment. We were able to see how creative they were and their ability to think on the spot, because that obviously would come into play in the role. We could see how they worked in a kitchen environment with other chefs, which you don't normally get to see first when you are recruiting chefs. You may get to see them do a test or a trial, but you don't get to see the interplay.

We were able to see all of those wonderful little pieces of engagement that you see when people are working in a team, albeit a team that was thrown together for the first time. We ran that four times during the day and those successful applicants formed our pre-opening and opening BOH team. The front of house experience was also interesting, because we were still setting up our SOPs. We decided this was a perfect opportunity for these applicants to actually get involved in developing several procedures to operate this 150-seat venue.

A lot of thought and attention to detail went into ensuring we could extract some tangible SOPs from the open audition day in order to get some of our processes set. There were three different experiences. The first was a blind taste test. They weren't expecting this, and it was wonderful to see their reactions when they were blindfolded. We ensured that everyone got the same amount of food to taste and identify. We were generous to begin with, comparing the likes of peanut butter versus strawberry jam versus smashed avocado. Then we moved into cheddar cheese, brie, stilton, before finally getting a little more adventurous with cumin, paprika, tumeric. I think if memory serves, we finished it off with tomato ketchup just to mess with their minds a little. It was fun but also as we were a food-driven concept, it was important that the guys on the floor understood the types of ingredients that were going into these dishes.

Then we gave them a blank, four-top table with no crockery, cutlery, glassware, table linen or mats. We opened a pantry full of resources that included different table mats, table cloths, candles, roses, salt and pepper sets, knives, forks, spoons, glassware and more. The challenge here was to set a table in two minutes in what they believed a MasterChef, the TV Experience table would look like, letting their creativity flow. For us, we could see if the direction we were going in was similar to the expectations of the candidates auditioning to work with us. Some people had the impression that, if it's that brand, then it needs to be a white tablecloth with silverware and high stem glasses and a beautiful rose in a single long stemmed vase. We didn't go in that direction instead going for an industrial minimalistic feel, in keeping with making the food the showcase. It was impressive to see how many of the candidates went in that direction on the day as well.

Lastly we did speed interviews. It was five minutes, and every person had a speed interview with myself, the head chef, the restaurant's general manager, the head of human resources and our PR manager. All of our questions were different but focused on specific needs of the roles we were recruiting allowing us to extract more of the personality of the individual. And that was our auditioning process to get our initial core team.

It wasn't a set of psychometric exams. It wasn't a reference check for people that they'd worked with before. We really went out on a limb, but decided that we needed to have the best in class for engagement with the guests and they needed to execute that on a day-to-day basis. I've used the same audition process since then and have found it to be a great tool, especially for front-facing individuals. Requesting a one minute video telling me why you want to come and work for me in this venue has also proven to be a bulletproof way of seeing a person's personality in a short space of time. Efficient and effective.

Hiring higher

To be successful in hospitality, we have to hire people. We can't do all of these roles we have been talking about ourselves. I haven't been a restaurant manager or an operations manager for many years. Sure, I can still do it if

CREATE TO PLATE

I have to, but there are so many people out there better at it than me, with updated knowledge and skills that it just makes sense to hire them. With our most recent restaurant that we opened in Australia, Vesper Bistro and Bar, I wanted a core team of people that could absolutely support the vision that we had for our Mediterranean island concept. I have to say, that in all of the years that I've been working in hospitality, it was here in Australia that I got to work with two of the greats. Our team, Francesco and Valeria proved to be completely invaluable. Valeria is an operations magician, on top of and in control of every single element. She just encapsulated what we were creating and made it seem effortless. Even though on certain nights things felt on the brink of collapse, Valeria knew the state of play with the kitchen and every table on the floor, far more than I did. That's why you bring people into your team that are better at doing their job than you are.

She also had a fascinating appreciation of wines and was committed to grow her knowledge where possible. Now, I love my wines and I have a broad understanding, but her attention to detail and ability to curate the portfolio of wines on our list that complemented the food concept surpassed any list I could have assembled at the time. Chef Francesco was instrumental in the curation of the menu – he understood the brief and created a menu perfectly reflecting the ideation of the outlet. He did his research and he executed these dishes with finesse and amazing creativity and attention to detail.

I know some people will say, 'I can't have people better at the job than me. They'll start telling me what to do!' You know what? That's okay if they have great ideas for your business. You need to set up the boundaries of working as a team. Ensure you establish a place and time when all ideas can be shared. We learn from our sharing of ideas and hearing from others. Some will be good, some not so good. Sometimes their ideas may be better than yours. Embrace them, it's for the betterment of the business. I can tell you many examples of where we've agreed and when we've agreed to disagree, the main thing is that the right idea will be the one that gets implemented.

Hiring the right people for your business is also critical. It's often far more costly to bring in the wrong person to fill the role. I know this because I've done it myself.

I'll give you an example where I have rushed in and it has failed me. Firstly, the situation was that I just needed people on the floor. However, I quickly realised that while these people were costing me X amount of dollars an hour, they couldn't carry two plates, let alone three! The extra work that needed to be done to serve a table of six, three trips back to the kitchen, rather than two, created inefficiencies. This meant the guests didn't get the same level of service that they would've, had it been done by someone else, or even myself at that stage. I learnt it's not just about hiring the people you need, because need implies desperation or survival. Instead, hire the people you want and take take the time to find the right ones.

Another tip is to choose team members who have connections and know what is happening in the industry, so that if you have a situation where you're down on staff for whatever reason, they'll know someone they can call who they trust that can come in and step into that role and help you out. The ultimate success of a business really does rely solely on the people.

CREATE TO PLATE

The dangers of over-promotion

Another thing that has unfortunately crept into the industry over the last 10 years is rapid over-promotion. This can be disastrous, not just for yourself, but for the person involved. I interviewed a candidate for a role as a general manager of an outlet, a substantial outlet. When I asked how many years of experience they had as a GM, they said 18 months. When I asked what their role was before that, they said they were a restaurant supervisor in a relatively mid-sized operation. When the GM of the venue left, the owner automatically promoted this supervisor to GM, and it was too much too soon. They got completely overwhelmed and couldn't manage the day-to-day needs of the business with the GM's hat on. They promptly left and started applying for GM roles in other businesses, but the issue was, that they hadn't had the training, time or ability to develop the skill sets needed to execute that role because they'd been over-promoted way too quickly.

I think this happened because it was just easier for the employer to do that, than it was to go out and find the right person for the role. I even see it in kitchens now, where chefs are coming in wanting to be a head chef on a substantial amount of money and they're only in their early twenties. They haven't had the experience of being a junior sous chef or chef de partie and moving up through the ranks. They just want to jump those steps, and we are all guilty of doing that at times. However, if you are opening your business, learn from the mistakes of others.

The fact is, that hiring the right person in the very beginning will always save you money and will cost you less in the long run.

The importance of a fast fire

The last part I need to touch on is firing fast. Yes, it sometimes can be hard to let people go, but it does happen in our business. I need to be very clear with this. The longer you keep someone around in your organisation that is a bad egg or is not performing, the greater the negative impact that it has on everyone else within your team. It's quicker just to get them out and replace them than to keep trying to fix the problem.

We work in the personality business and I've tried to give as many tips and ideas here about how you can see the interplay between people during the recruitment process, to make sure that they do work together, but it is critical that if a member of your staff for some reason doesn't fit, you move them on and put someone in that does. I know there will be those of you that say, 'Duncan, I just need people on the floor. I can't do it all myself.' There are those times when the industry is a little light on available resources. I absolutely appreciate that, but you know what? My suggestion is to take the time to find the right person. Even if as a stopgap, you need a casual to fill, never stop looking for the people you want, never stop looking. If there's a position that's available, that you have filled with someone that may not be up to the mark, but they fill a need, don't stop recruiting. Just find the right person and change them out.

I know that some of you are going to say 'he or she is a bit of a troublemaker, but I just can't fire them'. Let me stand here and say, yes, you can fire them. They are affecting the success and sustainability of your business. You need to remove them like expired food because they are creating more harm than good and potentially damaging the work of the good people, the fine people, the people that you have invested all of your time and effort in recruiting and training. They are potentially bringing them down. Take the hard decisions when you need to, and make it happen. I promise you, it will be good for your business in the long run.

ACTION

List down the 3 key personality traits you look for in any person you would like to work with.

SLAM DUNK!

'Always hire based on personality. You can teach the rest.'

CHAPTER 9

LAUNCH PAD TO SUCCESS

'The most successful restaurants in your city can't survive one single day without marketing.'

Mark Khoder

So you are now ready to open the doors and blast off! Let's first make sure that you have put all the pieces in place to effectively launch your new venue into the market and get people knocking down your door.

As a new venue, you only get one chance at making an amazing first impression. Preparation and planning well ahead of your opening date is key, and by scheduling and aligning multiple marketing activities to occur simultaneously, you will get the most impact. You want to generate a buzz amongst your identified target market that commands attention and gets people curious and excited to try you. After all, the ultimate goal is to kickstart your business by enticing first-time diners and getting bums on seats – and then getting them to spread the word. As we all know, the most powerful form of advertising in hospitality is positive word of mouth, even expressed digitally (I'm referring to you Tik Tok), with referrals shared within family, friends, business and social networks.

Every new venue's ultimate success will really depend on the unique selling points (USPs) that sets your concept, as a whole, apart from your competitors, both in your local community as well as in the wider market place. Once you have identified all the key strengths of your location, opening hours, interior design, cuisine style, quality and selection of food and beverage, signature dishes, pricing, staffing personality and knowledge. Then created your branding to reflect these attributes in your venue name, signage, uniforms, menus, photography, website, social and sales collateral, you are ready to reach out to the world of patrons with clear and targeted messaging to give people compelling reasons to try you.

However, there is another key ingredient that is a must to highlight in your initial and ongoing messaging – yes you have heard it a few times before … you need to create an 'emotional connection' with your venue by telling your own story. Hospitality is a very human business and it makes all the difference when people understand your motivation and values, and how this is reflected in your venue. Sharing what is important to you, and why, resonates with people on an emotional level and will entice them to want to have that 'feel' good experience.

When opening Vesper Bistro and Bar, we created an amazing connection with our diners based on our story. We shared the meaning and origin of our venue name, spoke about our passion and many travels to the Med and how we personally felt when dining at these beautiful islands. Our desire was to evoke that same feeling in our venue which was well suited to this theme with a floral wallpaper canopy and lovely outdoor courtyard and flowing fountain. We spoke about how much we loved being in a relaxed European setting, enjoying a leisurely meal with no time pressure. The fresh seafood and dishes full of colour and flavour, the warmth of the staff, lively social atmosphere, friendly community, receiving a warm welcome by the owner and being in a place that makes you feel special. Our story and passion resonated with so many people who could identify with their own memories of their travels and experiences. Just be sure that when you share your story, you can deliver on your promise!

Know your ideal customer

Your objective at the launch of your business is to ensure you are speaking with and reaching your ideal target market. Therefore it is important to truly understand all the characteristics about your ideal diner so you can engage and influence them. This includes not only where they live, their age, gender, income level, social interests, marital status, education, employment and disposable income, but also, importantly, their personality! Are they extroverts, people that like to party with their friends? Or fashionistas who like to be seen? Or, are they an older crowd who like to dine early and don't enjoy loud noise? What's their motivation for going out? Do they enjoy romantic nights out, casual family gatherings or dining in groups with friends?

As discussed previously, a venue can certainly attract various target markets for different times of the day as well. For you, this may include a breakfast or lunch crowd, pre-dinner drinks or dinner, as well as groups attending events.

Once you clearly understand who your audience is, it will be much easier to communicate with them in the right tone of voice and style, whether you are fun or formal, humorous, cheeky or super friendly and casual. Share what you offer, in a language that describes qualities that appeal to their taste buds, imagination, comfort and status. Be guided by the knowledge of who you are speaking to in order to formulate your key marketing messages, taglines in your copywriting and also reflect this in the images you use. This will clearly affect how you're positioned and perceived amongst your competitors.

Launch success

Okay, now you are ready to go! The question you may be asking at this point is, do I need to spend money on a launch? Isn't word of mouth free and still the best form of marketing in hospitality? Yes, 100%, positive word of mouth is still one of the most effective ways to generate referrals and return visits. However, to get the most impact at the time you open and generate a good flow of new guests, you need to make sure that you are making a big splash. Glowing customer satisfaction and reviews will always be your best PR that's for sure, but you need to get the word out to let people know you are open for business and ready to impress.

So, if you're ready to launch, where do you start? When planning a launch for maximum impact, these are some of the main elements you'll need to consider:

Professional photography Invest in high resolution images for your launch (landscape for media). You will need to capture a combination of food shots, staff in action and design elements that relay the look and feel of the venue. It's more than bricks and mortar. It's a living, breathing, feeling entity that provides a sensory experience through design, colour, artwork, food, people and space. You can use these images to promote your business on your website, social platforms, and via any future media opportunities that arise.

Public relations PR is any interaction that gets your business in front of the right audience with a large following. This can be achieved through a short or long-term engagement of a PR agency who will utilise their media network to create some buzz and excitement about your opening. This will typically involve sending out a press release to secure press coverage in the most relevant media, along with an invitation to food writers to dine in and publish a review. Your PR agent may also create opportunities to appear in podcasts, in local print and online publications, and social networks.

They can also organise an opening/launch event with influential media representatives and people in the community such as business leaders, celebrities and professional influencers who will share their experience with their followers. Media coverage like this can deliver a boost of mass awareness and be a very effective way to reach a high volume of people who are interested in food, dining and events, and are guided by media opinions and recommendations through articles, best new restaurants lists, hot new openings and other types of publicity. This will have both an immediate impact at the time of opening and also more long lasting exposure as details of the venue publicity remains visible online. When people search or view the web, they will likely still be able to find your listing for months to come.

Influencers Social influencers online have become a very important part of a hospitality marketing strategy. These individuals often have a passion for food or related areas and have managed to generate thousands of followers – people who are interested in what they say and do, who follow their recommendations. It is worthwhile reaching out to relevant influencers and invite them to your venue. Some may require upfront payment, while others you can invite them to dine or have an experience in exchange for agreed deliverables to their database (e.g. one video story and three social posts with photos and text to their network) in order to spread the word far and wide.

Local community Tap into your local community and business databases for support with your launch. Be sure to contact the local business association, as they may re-post your details in their newsletters or social feeds. Local businesses are generally open to support their neighbours, and can recommend you to their staff, colleagues and clients as a gesture of good will.

Business partnerships Work on creating partnerships that align with your venue's brand. Make sure that the partnership provides both parties with value. Connect with local businesses and offer to sponsor their event with a prize (like a dining or bar voucher to your venue) and they may support you by providing access to their customer base to spread the word. This could be a book shop having an event, a retail outlet that needs a venue for a launch of their new fashion label, a nearby real estate agent that wants to take their team to lunch, a business association that has regular social gatherings and needs to refer venues, a wedding fashion retailer that will refer your venue to clients, a beauty brand that is willing to sponsor your Mother's Day or a special theme night ... the list of partner opportunities is endless. Reach out, get involved, create relationships and you will find the cycle will create an amazing avalanche of referrals.

A recent example demonstrates this in action. Our venue's target demographic were women and as a result, we aligned ourselves with DIOR beauty and a number of other popular fashion and retail businesses to promote at our launch events. This helped to attract interest, boost brand positioning and ultimately, created bookings.

Local events Take part in relevant local and city-based events, such as food and wine festivals, street fairs, theme days, any activity that involves you being profiled amongst your competitors and gets you exposure in your community.

Trade partnerships Subscribe and gain inclusion into related marketing sales programs that will feature and list your venue so you can capitalise on the exposure to their databases such as restaurant gift card programs, wedding portals and event referral services.

Family and friends' networks Your own network of family and friends should be a great resource for getting support and feedback. Invite them to food trials and host a pre-opening launch evening for them to do a test run of staff, service and food and get any feedback before opening the doors to the public. They are probably your greatest supporters and by reaching out to their own communities on socials, they can provide you with immediate access to a group of followers and new diners.

In one of our previous venues featuring Mediterranean island cuisine, we had a focus on Greek dishes. As a result of a visit from a friend of our team, a high profile Greek celebrity chef, and a social post with his recommendation to over 450,000 of his followers on Instagram, we had an instant boost in our Insta followers and a regular flow of the Greek community coming in to try our venue because of the trust they had in his opinion. It's not something that you can buy. It has to be part of a genuine exchange of support.

Networking groups Aligning yourself with the right networking organisations is also a great way to reach your target client and introduce your venue to first time customers. As a Mediterranean Island concept, we created an alliance with many of the European Chambers of Commerce (French, Italian, Greek, etc.) as well as niche networking groups such as the 'European Women in Business' which attracted the right demographic as our shared cultural interest encouraged their members to support us.

Reservations booking platform Utlitise this platform to feature your NEW venue to their database and be sure to be listed and appear in all marketing or re-targeted communications via email, socials, website, etc.

Website Set up a Google Business page and help people searching on Google to find you by boosting your SEO (search engine optimisation). Upload images, events, menus, experiences, using keywords that may appear in a search to enable potential customers to find you based on their criteria. Use Google Analytics and optimisation tools to monitor and measure the results.

So I hear you say, 'Well, that's great. It's good to do all of those things, but what if I don't have a big budget for a launch?' Not everyone does have the budget to spend on creating a huge launch event or the many marketing activities that go with it. Well, I think if you don't have the budget, there are still a number of ways to launch your business without spending big. It's about smart and well-designed social media campaigns with good photography and videos, inviting friends and family to pre-opening events and hosting a good list of influencers. Tell the story behind the creation, the why, let people see your belief, passion, and enthusiasm for what you have to offer. All this can still generate good results, especially when done alongside sourcing media opportunities and alliances with local community organisations. Of course, you can also be your own walking, talking PR machine, and it is 100% free!

CREATE TO PLATE

ACTION

Identify the 5 key actions you will take to launch your venue.

SLAM DUNK!

'Marketing is the enticement, the introduction and the tease, how you position yourself through your branding and PR – this is why people will ultimately choose your venue.'

CHAPTER 10

YOUR PRESENCE = YOUR PREENT

'Focus on your customers and lead your people as though their lives depend on your success.'

Warren Buffet

Believe it or not, as the owner or manager of the business, your customers actually want to meet you. I know crazy, right? But when you're in this game called the hospitality industry, there is an in-built desire to connect with the people behind the creation of a new venue. They want to understand what drives us, where our inspirations came from and meet the person that has created this amazing venue, and if you're an operator, they want to understand the story behind your creation.

They also want to give you some really valuable feedback. For you, this is an opportunity to both build a personal connection with your guests, as well as gather important data on your customers' preferences, such as how they discovered you and what impresses them. You can motivate them to review and rate their experience online, learn valuable information on what is working, and gain insight into how you can improve along the way.

In business, we want to collect as much data as possible on the good, the bad and the indifferent for our establishment. Some people invest money in their venues but they never invest their time in them. A good friend of mine, who owns multiple venues, is in at least one of his outlets every day, because that's where he gets to see what's going on with guests and with his team. So, it's hugely important to be in the venue, not sitting in an office, not looking at reports, but be on the ground. You'll gather so much valuable information that you can then use for marketing purposes, for potential menu changes, or just simply hear feedback on what you're doing right and what a fantastic experience guests are having.

Some of the things that I have suggested you implement throughout this book will give the operations team the power to avoid complaints, such as the systems in your operations bible. When you are on the floor, you have the power to deal with complaints before or as they occur. We will go through ways that you can do that. As an owner, there's a huge benefit of seeing is believing, not relying on third party feedback or getting a report at the end of the night from your GM or your restaurant or bar manager. You're actually physically there seeing what's going on.

Then of course, there is understanding the conversion of your presence into dollars. How is it that you being on the floor can impact your ability to make more money? Operators can easily lose control of their venue if they spend too much time off the floor. For some, the realisation of this can be too late.

When you are not present for extended periods of time, when you've created this concept and then you go and sit in an office during service periods not witnessing what's happening, your venue can go off the rails very quickly indeed. It takes a lot of work, effort and resources to get it back on track.

It's so important for you to be visible and engaged during service periods, during night shifts, whenever it is customer facing times. Not all of the time, but some of the time, and that's true in any business environment. But again, specifically relating to hospitality, when guests can get to speak and interact with the owner, they feel special and appreciate the recognition of their custom and loyalty. They feel seen and valued and this makes a huge difference. Not only will this impact their personal connection with the venue but they generally share this positive experience in reviews and return visits ... with friends!

Being mindfully present

Now, you may argue and say, 'I've hired the right people. I'm paying them good money. I don't need to be there,' but you run the risk of losing control of your business. You will stop inspiring your team. They will be left to their own inspiration and to interpret what it is they believe you want without having your input.

You'll also not have the opportunity to hear directly from your guests. You will get feedback, but it will be third party feedback. And sometimes it will be positioned or skewed a certain way.

You will not see which areas need to be addressed in the successful performance of your business. When you're in the room, you see everything that you've built. You might need to make a modification to a system that's in the operations bible because you see your staff keep bumping into each other when they're crossing the floor. Maybe your table layout isn't in the right place to allow for maximum circulation for guests going to the bathroom. All of these things you don't see or hear, or experience, unless you're in the venue.

It's not about you necessarily doing anything specific in the venue. You do have people engaged to do that. How do we do this then, without stepping on the feet of the people that we have working for us and with us? I know, I've done this before. Once you've hired an amazing team of people, it's very important that you don't take over their role. You don't want to undermine their authority or take over the job that you've hired them to do.

It comes down to a few very simple things. Firstly it's about scheduling. Knowing who's doing what. It's common knowledge that as a business owner, we have more to do than just serve our guests, but we need to do this outside of service hours. Looking at reports and profit and loss statements, analysing your food and beverage costs, fine-tuning your marketing strategies, these are insights into what has occurred in the past. During operational hours, we get to be involved in what's happening in the present! You have hired extremely capable people to run the venue and your presence is there to support it, not to take it over. So the key learning here is to have clearly defined job descriptions and roles so you can be present on the floor without stepping on other people's toes. And then you need to support them. You don't change them. If you've got an amazing restaurant manager, let them run the show.

Now, if I was to come onto the floor to support the venue in any which way that I could, or to engage with guests, I would do that around the service points. So a classic example, one of our waitstaff is welcoming the table, which is where we basically take the first drinks orders and engage the guests on the dining journey that they will be taking with us. There may be some menu specials and options to discuss or some market pricing that needs to be addressed, this is the key introduction of that staff member to the table and their first point of contact. That is not the time for you to go and engage with the guests. There are moments that permeate through the guests' journey, where natural gaps occur in the sequence of service. That is the perfect time to engage with the guests.

You may have a system for executing the first round of drinks order. In that environment, right at the very beginning, there is the opportunity for an upsell to a special wine by the glass, a cocktail or a beer. If the owner arrives at the table, before the waiter has had the chance to introduce themselves and get that first drink order, and offers 'Let me arrange a welcome drink for you.' Boom, you've lost money. Now you may have done it with the absolute greatest intention, but you've removed a critical piece of the service program, which is when that waiter gets to have that first encounter with the guest and gets to upsell what might be available on the day.

CREATE TO PLATE

Let's assume you are running your wines under the Coravin system and you have a bottle that has been open for a few days that you want to promote up and move. Your generous actions have potentially removed an opportunity for an upsell and better cost management.

Your engagement needs to be tailored and structured. In my experience, if a restaurant manager ever needed assistance on the floor, then I wouldn't take over their job and make them do the other elements of service. If, for instance, I came onto the floor and there was a lot of pressure on the kitchen, or there were plates building up on the pass and not getting delivered to the table, then I would jump in and run the plates. I'll clear the tables, I'll pour the wine, but I wouldn't come in and take over the role of someone that you have hired, who is better at their job than you are. I'll go in and fill the gaps.

There are times when the guests at the table may be at the end of a meal when they're having dessert or you are clearing their table. This is an opportunity to engage and you can introduce yourself as the owner. They may have no idea and zero expectation that you would be doing this job so it becomes one of those really nice surprise moments where guests state, 'Oh my gosh, we're having the owner clear our table.' Now it's not every day that these things happen, but when it does happen, it creates an amazing opportunity to personally connect with your guests. Once everything quietens down, they might want to know, how long have you been in the business? What was your motivation to feature this type of cuisine? What's the story behind the venue? They may talk about their favourite dish or 'what an amazing chef and team you've got!' and you get all of that feedback from the ground up. You're not trying to wait for a report at the end of the night that talks about the service and the way that it occurred. You're getting that on the ground face to face feedback, which is invaluable to tailoring and tweaking your offering for continually meeting and exceeding your guests' expectations. It does make a huge difference.

Wearing different hats

I was the Head of Clé Restaurant & Bar and in charge of one of the biggest restaurant openings that Dubai had ever seen. When I say big, it was BIG! We did the opening over two nights with entertainment by Cirque de Soleil, food by Michelin starred chef Greg Malouf, and hosted celebrity guests which included Paris and Nicky Hilton, Khloe Kardashian, Creative Director of Balmain, Olivier Rousteing, supermodels Alessandra Ambrosio and Irina Shayk, Heads of State, government and captains of industry, many Bollywood actors including Hrithik Roshan, and Akon was there as well. It was huge. There were 800 people each night all enjoying free pouring of Dom Pérignon champagne and it was phenomenal, an amazing experience!

Once the venue opened, I spent all of my time on the floor during service hours. In any business there are times when you end up wearing multiple hats, whether you are an operator or the owner-operator of a business. These were the hats that I wore during the opening of that particular venue.

On opening night, at four o'clock in the afternoon, the venue is ready to go, everyone is pumped to the max and … the air conditioning fails.

CREATE TO PLATE

The opening party was a sit down dinner for the first night and then a dance party the second night. So I had to put on my problem solver hat … I had to source 10 mobile air conditioning units to fill a space of about 12,500 square feet. Sourcing the units was hard enough but the building did not have the power to support them.

We found a company that could deliver us a generator, which we sunk into a construction pit next to the venue, within two hours, to power these air conditioning units that we had to have installed. When the units arrived, they were taupe in color and the venue was black. Not a good look, so we then spray painted them all black and hid them inconspicuously around the venue. Problem solved! We addressed that particular issue so that by the time the event came to fruition, the venue was cool. It was held in October in Dubai, when it was still very warm outside, but in the end we had ensured a comfortable temperature for all.

At no point in time did I take over the role of the general manager who was running the show that night. No. I organised the air conditioning myself, so the GM and the team could continue preparing for the event and be ready for when those first brand new guests walked through the door.

To top it all off, Paris Hilton jumped up behind the decks and did an off the cuff DJ set, which was fantastic for the launch of the venue (you can see a video of this at thecuttingedgeagency.com). As a result of that impromptu act, my role transitioned again and I put on my security hat. We had no big security people there. So myself and a couple of other rather substantial men surrounded the DJ desk to provide a barrier while Paris was DJ'ing. Again at no point in time, did I get the general manager involved. That was not his job on the night.

Rather than pulling someone out of the role that you have carefully crafted for them, and then hired them to do, you do those extra things yourself, and it makes for a much more seamless experience.

We'd never expected the air conditioning not to be able to support the volume of people in the room. These are things that you discover and can solve when you're on the floor, not things that you want to see in a report the following day.

During the launch for 'Intersect' by Lexus, we had the general manager running the show, and I was there in support on the launch night. We were very fortunate to have Mark Ronson come and perform 'Uptown funk', which had only just been released with Bruno Mars.

Intersect is a moderate venue in size and Mark was up on this very small platform, with hundreds of people surrounding him while he's doing his set. Some even jumping up on the podium and wanting to have a dance with him. And you could just see he was becoming uncomfortable with what was happening. Maybe security was my calling, as my job was to make sure that we had people there to create a barrier for him. And the general manager continued on with making sure that every guest was served with beautiful drinks, amazing samples of our food, and the music went on and everyone had a great night.

Being in the venue, this is where you get to make these snap decisions and your service and your guest experience can continue to run unhindered.

Solve problems before they happen

I mentioned before that this is also a crucial opportunity for you to use your power, to avoid complaints or to mitigate potentially extenuating circumstances. A great example of this is when you get to approach a table of guests and gauge where they are at and what the mood is like. Feedback is one thing but seeing the consumption, is another. Has everyone completed all their dishes? Is there a lot of food left? If you notice a side dish that hasn't been touched, you get to ask, 'I noticed that you haven't touched your salad niçoise, is there something I can do about that now for you?' rather than waiting until the end of a meal, where they leave and state 'that salad nicoise was not up to par' and then proceed to post a review about it online. You get to mitigate that because you get to become the be all and end all of problem-solving.

Where guests are at their most vulnerable and your business is at its most vulnerable, is when there is a problem, a concern, or potential for a complaint when something hasn't gone right. Usually, they will talk to your waiter. They will then talk to your restaurant manager and then it escalates to you at times. If you're there, it can go directly to you first and you can address it then and there. What could have been an explosive problem becomes nothing more than a misunderstanding.

Your power and ability, without detracting from any of the other roles and responsibilities of your team on the floor, is the conversion of your presence on the floor to more dollars in your pocket. You know, those guests may never have come back again, but because you have handled the situation personally and have the power, as the owner, it was resolved immediately. If you want to give away the entire top shelf of the bar to a table that's upset with their service, that's within your power. It's not within the power of the people that you've hired. It's not their job. Converting your presence into dollars can also lead to more revenue in the future by building loyalty and potential for repeat customers, which as we know is the best form of revenue that you can have coming in, because once you've got them in there's no marketing dollars spent to get them back.

I've been told that sometimes I look like a godfather when I'm in one of my venues and that's because I will find a focal point where I can see and observe the entire room. That's when I get to gauge the times to go and approach each table. I'm not standing next to the tables. I'm not standing next to people waiting for them to finish a conversation. I'm reading the room from afar. That is a powerful tool in hospitality, because seeing the room and then going through the room and making your approaches at the right time is seamless and effortless, when you do it right.

Maybe you think hospitality is a real passion of yours, but you're not really a people person. I will challenge that, because hospitality is a people business, whether it's guests, employees, contractors, or suppliers, we're always dealing with people. I encourage you to think about the interaction from the guests' perspective. How would you feel if the owner of the venue came and spoke to you? When you wear the guest hat and think about the warmth and the feeling of importance that guest has when the owner of the venue comes and engages and really shows care and authenticity around your experience and feedback, it's easy to see why this matters.

CREATE TO PLATE

ACTION

Plan your office/BOH work schedule so that you can be present in the venue during service periods.

SLAM DUNK!

'There's nothing more special for a guest than having the owner genuinely and authentically engaged with them and making them feel important.'

CHAPTER 11

THE KEYS TO LONGEVITY

'Consistency is better than perfection. We can all be consistent. Perfection is impossible.'

Michael Hyatt

Consistency is key throughout this journey of creating our amazing ultimate concept with soul.

One of the biggest learnings or insights I can give you from all the years I've been doing this is that consistency is key to your financial success. Why do I say that? Well, repetition breeds relevance. Why is that the case? We will explore in this chapter learning the value of consistent service in food and beverage offerings, and in your on-brand marketing. We'll also unpack the importance of understanding your guest expectations on a referral visit and their expectations on a second visit, and how this differs.

The value of consistent service When we talk about consistency in service, we're referring to the delivery, in other words, what we're putting out for our guests. This means making sure that our approach to guests and sequence of service is consistent with each visit, with every dish served the same way each time. The contents and ingredients are prepped, cooked and plated in the same way, and then executed at the table in the same way.

The value of consistent on-brand marketing We need the story that we put out in the marketplace around who we are and what we do to remain consistent. We're not chopping and changing. We're not picking different markets. We're staying true to the market that we've chosen and the demographic that we've chosen. We are continuing to appeal to our customer profile.

Understanding your guest expectations on referral visits These guests are coming to you because of your word of mouth marketing. They've heard someone raving about your venue and now they want to check it out. Obviously they have some expectations based on what they've heard from others. What are they going to see, hear, touch, feel and smell when they come to your venue?

Your guest expectations on their second visit What are they expecting when they come back? Believe it or not, consistency actually builds trust with your guests, enhances your reputation and can ultimately contribute directly to your profitability. Adversely, the cost of inconsistencies in delivery of hospitality can become exorbitant.

Consistency is key. Food and beverage cost consistency and delivery means efficiency and less wastage, and that contributes greatly to the overall bottom line.

What can happen if we are inconsistent?

You're opening the doors ready to deliver on your promise – but then you fail to deliver on the expectations, from a consistency point of view. Your food is inconsistent. Your service is inconsistent. Your marketing is inconsistent. These will all lead to financial disaster. It's much better to make sure that when you do start, you prioritise consistency and execute this at that highest level, now and into the future. Remember, it's not about perfection. Consistency is more achievable and produces greater results in the long run. If you don't do this, you run the risk of irreparable damage to your reputation. You'll see an obvious decrease in repeat customers and repeat patronage. People won't be getting the same product every time they go and you'll be spending more money to attract new customers. You want to invest in marketing up-front to bring people through the door and then the experience that they receive and what you generate for them within the venue is what makes them want to come back. Every time those experiences fail to meet or exceed our guests' expectations, we then need to spend more money attracting new customers. When we fail to deliver, we might even need to compensate guests, which will result in further financial losses.

Finally, being inconsistent is an unviable long-term situation. You're not going to last. It's not going to allow you to deliver on your concept, and this will hurt your profitability and hinder your success. The guests will not receive what they expect and ultimately, they will look elsewhere to other establishments who can deliver.

If you look at the term consistency, by definition, it is the quality of always behaving or performing in a similar way.

In hospitality, we're basically talking about delivery of a product. We are in the product delivery business, in the service business, and it's about setting a standard for that delivery, and then ensuring that we continue to execute that delivery at that same standard.

When you think about it, everything you've done in this journey to get to this point is based on delivering a consistent product. Each step we've taken, from concept brief to the design to the operations bible, is all about delivering and executing a consistent product. You've invested all this time in breaking down each and every single procedure throughout the customer journey, so that it can be delivered in a particular way, so that your guests can experience and enjoy your concept with soul. You're investing time in training staff, in ensuring that each one of your recipes is considered and thought out, down to the last pinch of salt, to make sure that the finished product is prepared to an exacting standard.

You're no longer in the design phase now. You are absolutely dealing with guests coming into the venue and parting with their hard-earned money in order to experience what it is that you have to offer. Hence why I have dedicated an entire chapter to focus on consistency. It's so important and it really impacts your ability to run your business effectively and to futureproof your operations.

Consistency in your brand

From a success point of view, consistency can be measured in many ways. I've talked briefly about food and service, but consistency in your message, story and brand is also essential. Using the MasterChef, the TV Experience example again, when we worked with Banijay Group, I experienced firsthand that consistency in messaging was key, right from the very early stages. Every single stakeholder was involved in the messaging that was going out, because there were specific ways we needed to convey our wording to be on brand. For example, there was a simple advertisement where the location of the logo was deemed to be acceptable by the brand owner, but not acceptable by others.

Consider this when building your brand. Look for consistency whenever your brand is used or shared. For every social media post that you put out there, choose where on the post your logo will be positioned (e.g. bottom left or top right) use your brand colours and font to consistently deliver visuals that show uniformity. If visitors look at all of your stories, social posts, promotional materials and email newsletters, the brand elements are consistent and easily identifiable. They are not darting all over the place, subconsciously disrupting the flow of message in the mind of your guest. This makes a huge difference to the authenticity of your product.

If you're an upmarket casual eatery stay true to your positioning with imagery and language that reflect your venue and customer base ... don't create fine-dining high stemware posts. It's not relevant to you and it's not consistent with what you're producing. Ultimately, all it will do is create unrealistic expectations for potential guests.

A great example of this can be seen in gastro pubs, which, have seen phenomenal growth over the last 10 to 15 years. There's a set expectation as to what the food, beverage and service element will be. I'm not expecting, white floor length linen tablecloths and staff in ties. No, I'm expecting a really, good, casual environment, but high-end food and high-end service.

So, if you're producing or creating a gastro pub, it's important that you convey in your messaging a casual, refined concept. Focus on streamlining how you present the visual elements that reflect the venue and food, so you appeal to your market in a consistent tone of voice. Consistency and relevance in what you're putting forward from a marketing perspective is absolutely crucial.

This consistency in branding should also follow through once your guests are in the venue, including the design and language of the food and beverage menus, coasters, logos and colours of staff uniforms.

Consistency in your delivery

Coming back to food, you have invested a lot of time in creating an operations bible and recipe systems, ensuring that each recipe is calculated out by ingredient, weight and cost. The reason we do this is so that if you have to execute 10 beef wellingtons, then each beef wellington should be the same because it doesn't matter which guest is in the venue, they should be able to talk to someone else and relay exactly the same experience.

Look at cocktails too. A dry martini based on your recipe for a dry martini is your DRY MARTINI! And if that stays the same consistently then people know what to expect when they come to your venue. If they enjoy it and trust the consistency, they will refer you to their circle of influence. Then, when the people they have referred come to your venue and order that cocktail, they too will be expecting the same experience. A picture has been painted, when a referral takes place. It's a canvas and that canvas is painted by the guests that have had the experience and the person that they're talking to is the one who gets the impression of that canvas. They understand the artwork that is being created in front of them and when they arrive at the venue, they expect that canvas to match their impression. If it does, they too will become your brand ambassadors.

I said previously that personality is key in hospitality and you can train everything else. The importance in that training is to make sure that everyone is executing your concept to the same high standards. So the sequence of service, the service touchpoints where your staff are engaging with guests, the conversational pieces, the way to describe the specials – they all need to be consistent.

For those of you that are familiar with Australia, Pambula is a great location for oysters. But they do not always come from there, it will vary depending on seasonality. Knowledge is crucial, because if your guest enquires, 'Where are the oysters from today?' and your waitstaff say the wrong location, you're conveying a message of inconsistency to the guests which in turn can promote loss of faith, reputation and trust. A guest could say, 'If they don't know where the oysters are from how do we know they understand our allergy to nuts? Maybe they don't know which dishes have nuts in them either?' That's why the knowledge piece in delivery is so important because we all need to be speaking the same language. We all need to be sharing the same story.

Consistency is not just my opinion. The principle of consistency is one of the greatest keys to success in hospitality.

Some will inevitably say, 'Time is money. I just want to get them in, get them out, they need to spend to stay.' I appreciate that, but people will spend more if they receive a consistent product. One thing some operators don't realise is that the first touchpoint, the initial impressions are the things that build up a basis of what consistent service is going forward. So when your levels of consistency surpass the guests' expectations, you have a greater opportunity for increased sales.

Understand at this point in your journey that everything you do can lead to another sale, more choices and have an impact on amplifying the guest experience. Some of you will say, 'Surely people will have whatever I have made, because they have been here before.' Yes, some people will, but repeat customers are a gift. They are an absolute gift in business as we don't need to spend hard marketing dollars to attract them. Think about the fact that you've got a guest that comes back for a second, third or fourth time. The reason they're coming back is because you delivered at a level that met or exceeded their expectations. Trust me, they will expect that same level of delivery the next time they come.

What if you want to put something that is off-brand on your menu? Sometimes we see something new we'd like to try, or we may feel inspired to go a little bit outside the box. These are the people to test it out on before you commit. Give your repeat customers a dish that is off-brand, but give it to them complimentary, and they will give you honest, relevant feedback. It's an amazing litmus test to make sure you're still delivering consistently and on-brand. Put your idea out to your repeat customers as they have already bought into your concept. They may say, straight out, no. They may say, 'This is great Duncan, but not in this venue,' or, 'this actually compliments everything else that you're doing really well. Put it on the menu!'

You will recieve the honest feedback you need that will help you stay on-brand and continue to deliver consistently.

ACTION

List down the 3 consistent things you expect from your favourite venue.

SLAM DUNK!

'The fundamental worst-case scenario for any business is to invest everything you have up till now, and then let it all down by being inconsistent.'

CHAPTER 12

LIVING ON THE EDGE

'Chase the vision, not the money, the money will end up following you.'

Tony Hsieh

Congratulations, you've come this far! You've created an amazing concept with soul. Your doors are open. People are flocking in … but it's not over yet. We're always in a state of eternal growth, evolution and garnering greater knowledge. This is what will continually define you, your concept and your future concepts as market leaders and keep you ahead of the competition.

Why do we want to be ahead of our competition? That's our point of difference. That is where we create and establish our mark in society. Throughout this chapter, you will learn how to always keep yourself one step ahead of the competition, to have that competitive edge.

This is not new. People have been in the restaurant game for thousands of years, and it has been done before. If this is the start for you, there are a lot of learnings that you'll get access to and resources to assist you in the growth of your business that previously others didn't have. You've likely been so engrossed in what's happening within the four walls of your operation, you may not have had a chance to reflect. Remember to make time to work on your business, not always in your business. Now is the perfect time to stand back, look over the venue from a top down perspective and be inspired all over again ... and then continue to create, leverage and grow.

What can you do going forward that maybe in the original concept stage you didn't think about? What are some additional elements that you can put into your operation that will make it even more successful? Know that working on your business is growing your business. This is where we move from static to fluid. Whilst reviewing P&Ls, writing wine lists and preparing to get your cocktails made are all essential, they're based on what's already been done. This is where you are reflecting back on decisions that you've made in the past. Working on the business is where you look at how to position yourself going forward and define what you are going to do in the future

Never stop growing

Not working on the business means not being nimble or able to adapt to new situations. A great example of the need to adapt is the widespread impact of the recent global pandemic that we all experienced in one way or another.

LIVING ON THE EDGE

Lockdowns, closures and changes in operating conditions provided an opportunity for many to work on their business more, which allowed them to find ways to pivot, adapt and come up with new and exciting ways to continue to trade. Imagine what could happen if you just turned your creative mind on more and let the ideas flow.

Now that you're up and running, it's those inputs, the creativity, the flow, that have got you to this point. There's no need to now switch it off. You've got to keep your creative side nurtured. Keep feeding it new ideas, that will inspire you and your team.

If you don't steal with pride, you're not making the most of your unique opportunity – looking outside of your four walls and seeing what other people are doing is important. There will be some that are doing it really well and there's nothing wrong with taking good ideas and implementing them. Some of you might feel, it's not right to just take someone else's idea and implement it for my business. Use me as an example, I will happily share things that worked and didn't work for me over the last 30 plus years if it means you get a jump start in your hospitality business. These ideas are not proprietary and we have an industry that has grown due to the fact that common approaches to similar problems are shared. If you're not continuing to be creative, continuing to seek feedback and keeping your eye on the competition, you will not grow. And that would be terrible. Remember, most likely someone will take an idea that you have created and implemented during this process for themselves. Be proud of that.

When we say stay cutting edge, what does that actually mean? Why do I personally use that in my approach to the way I work? Cutting edge is about always being at the forefront of your venue, your competition and your market. You're prepared to take some risks for ultimate rewards. You utilise tried and tested tools to ensure you get the maximum out of your business.

Unique selling points are forever evolving, and this is a key element in ensuring you stay one step ahead and remain relevant. There comes a time as an established operation, which might be three or four years down the track, when you're thinking about version 2.0. Not wholesale change necessarily, but time to refresh things. We all do it in our personal lives too, where we want to paint a wall in our house, revive some outdoor furniture that's been in the sun for too long, or even visit a personal trainer, just to spice things up.

Sometimes people take the easy and more expensive route of complete wholesale change. I am not suggesting that you say, for example, 'Peruvian is not working for me anymore. Let's change the concept to Thai'. We hear this amongst industry chatter, but I'm here to tell you that before we submerge ourselves in the darkness of a complete rebuild, let's look at a refresh first. Let's look at version 2.0.

An outlet that we opened a few years ago just didn't hit the mark with the local community it was designed to engage with. It was a great concept – it was light, vibrant, solid, and yet the menu just didn't strike the right chord with its target audience. No fault of ours. We did the market research. We just couldn't get the audience to come in. We were getting influenced by many as to why this was happening. Some said the location was not right. We didn't have any hard (alcoholic) beverages available. It was a quirky design, and yet at the end of the day, it came down to one key issue. We just weren't relevant in the market that we were in. The outlet was not relevant to its local community, the menu was not relevant to the demographic. And as such, it suffered. The bones were good, but the dressing, what we were offering, needed work. So what we decided to do then was simplify the menu. The offerings were now tailored more to what the guests, our local Philippine community, wanted, and we had a mini rebirth of the venue. The changes received great feedback, but more importantly, great customer engagement. The name is the same. The location is the same, employer is the same. It was just version 2.0. And we were only able to do that because we stood outside of the business and looked in on it rather than working from within.

Focusing on one's relevance in society is an enormous undertaking, but it pays off an immense dividend when properly executed. This is a good time for egos to be checked at the door. For listening, not dictating, to what is being offered. It's inevitable that some hospitality venues ultimately won't succeed, but I'm here to tell you that does not have to be yours. Just because something worked in the past does not mean it is relevant in today's market. We have the same consumers with less in their pockets to spend. How do we address this? I'd like to challenge each and every one of you to step back from your business from time to time, look over it, rather than in it, and you might just see the next iteration of your existing venue peeking back at you as version 2.0.

When we opened and launched Vesper Bistro and Bar, we had an amazing menu offering. Through looking at it from the outside, rather than being in the business, we were able

CREATE TO PLATE

to see how we could entice people to try more of these dishes from the Mediterranean islands.

So we came up with a rethink on the traditional set menu concept. Now everyone has had a set menu, or a tasting menu or a degustation menu and these usually consist of multiple individual courses. Yes it has been done. What we wanted to do here was utilise a similar menu offering but instead of multiple courses there were multiple dishes, some shared and some individual. We called it the 'Vesperience'. This was a way for our consumers to have a selection of five or eight dishes from our à la carte menu and the offering was never the same day in, day out. It was a set price for each Vesperience menu, and our guests were able to experience more dishes at a perceived value for money entry into Mediterannean island dining. It proved to be hugely successful, some nights outweighing our à la carte offering. You can come up with new ideas and new strategies in order to improve your overall offering.

One of the other things that you get to do in this position is to invest in your senior team, as they're the ones who continue to drive sales. Just because you've bought them on board, and trained them up, it doesn't mean you then set and forget. These guys want to keep learning. They want to grow as well. You've hired passionate professionals for their personality. You've gone through all of those steps in the recruitment process that we talked about earlier. Now you need to look at what their values and goals are and support them with additional resources to grow their knowledge, either through coaching or online courses, WSET training and others. I've done that with my GMs before. They wanted to learn more about wine, so I sent them on the WSET course.

This new knowledge within your team is valuable as they can utilise their new skills with your guests. It allows you to keep growing and building your business, while also nurturing your team at the same time. For inspiration, you can view our online or face-to-face coaching and training services at thecuttingedgeagency.com

Investing in the team that you have working for you on the floor, in the bar or in the kitchen, gives you the opportunity to find new ways to build your business. Succession planning is also one of the great things that you can do when you're working on your business, identifying those high performers within your teams, both front and back of house, that you can see moving up through the ranks within your organisation. Seeing this early provides you with a great opportunity to tailor a program to develop their skills and knowledge and bring them up to speed. It could be a supervisor on the floor that you identify as a potential assistant restaurant manager in a couple of years time. How are you going to get them from where they are now to where you want them to be in the future? Looking down on your business from above and nurturing the talent from within, these are all soft skills that provide your employees with a strong desire to continue working with you. These are great opportunities for you as a hospitality venue operator to understand the needs and wants of your team and be able to tailor solutions for them throughout the course of their career with you. It really is that simple.

It's also a fantastic time to join or become part of an association that works closely with your industry. There are restaurant and catering associations across the globe, including the National Restaurant Association in the USA, the Restaurant and Catering Association of Australia and the UAE Restaurant Group, which has been established most recently, to name a few. I found it fascinating to be in this organisation at the inception stages when it was the Middle East Restaurant Association, and have enjoyed watching it grow to the powerhouse association it has become now. Within these groups is where you get to share a wealth of knowledge with your peers, and they with you. We all sometimes find ourselves in the position of having similar challenges and none of us have exactly the right answers. This opportunity to be part of your industry, to work with like-minded hospitality professionals and to listen and feed off one another through these associations, is a great way to find solutions to problems that you really thought were insurmountable.

Working on your business, being out there, networking with people that have been in the industry for many years, you continue to learn that these things work hand in hand. Connecting with a team that's already gone through this whole process, had all the learnings, and are able to provide you with additional skills, knowledge and experience that helps you become the best you can be is so valuable. We're not in this to operate in a silo. We're operating in an industry that has a huge amount of depth and breadth, and we need to leverage as much of that as possible in order to continue improving ourselves.

Improving our operations

You've heard me mention many times throughout this book, about creating a concept with soul. Let's now, for your own understanding, define soul again. It's the emotional and intellectual intensity associated with creativity. Soul is by definition a feeling and as such, this is how we should look at it. When we look to our hospitality operations, how do they make people feel? Take the opportunity to stand back and understand how your venue makes people feel, and make sure you continue to live on the edge. When all is said and done, if you want to be a pioneer then share your learnings with others. If you know a pioneer then ask, what do they do?

Don't be afraid to ask. Don't be reluctant to reach out. There are plenty of people, organisations, and support systems out there to help you grow and develop your business going into the future.

But hang on, a couple of chapters ago, you said, I need to be in my business. Now I'm out of my business. Which one is it? I'm confused! To be clear, I'm not expecting you to be doing the dishes or spending an entire shift in service. That's not my expectation. My suggestion is that your presence is there, but it's not about you physically doing service. This is where the venue is known to have the owner present and guests will provide feedback to you on that basis. That feedback can then form part of your growth strategies for the business.

Ultimately, the two operating entities work hand in hand. You are in the business, but also out. All I'm doing is highlighting that, you have a venue, so don't be locked down to a desk. That's not hospitality. I want you to imagine a new positioning statement for yourself. It will outline how you are going to avoid getting caught up in the day-to-day all the time, and be that leader in hospitality, that mentor, that pioneer, and continue to improve and grow, with potentially another venture or by further developing the one you have just completed.

We've reached the end, and I know this book has covered many topics. It is only the start of your journey. It is my approach to creating cutting-edge hospitality concepts. There is so much more out there for you to learn, discover and master, and importantly, so many more challenges to face. There are amazing people out there to assist you with it. So why not stay open and see what they can offer?

Remember these final words: 'If you remain cutting edge, you'll always be relevant. You'll always be authentic, and you'll always be able to deliver on your concept and your promise. And your public will thank you for it.'

ACTION

Reach out to me or my team for support, resources, training, case studies, and above all success strategies to keep you living and operating on the edge.

Start to build your concept with soul today.

SLAM DUNK!

'Innovation and forward thinking is critical. You cannot afford to just be in the business, because then you will stagnate and others will ultimately pass you.'

THE NEXT STEPS

The drive to create a new hospitality business starts with a fire in your belly, passion in your heart and a commitment to a vision.

After reading this book, you can see that it then takes creativity, project planning, financial acumen, people management, mentoring and training skills, an eye for design and function, creative problem-solving, negotiating with suppliers, understanding and complying with industry regulations and standards, branding, digital marketing and PR, customer relations and service. You have many hats to wear to manage and align all the moving parts along the way to achieving a successful outcome!

Most business owners tend to have some but not ALL of the specialised skills and so I hope that this book has provided you with some key insights, strategies and actions that you'll find useful and beneficial.

I have also included some offers for tools that you will find valuable to kick start your journey towards creating your amazing new venue.

Above all else, stay passionate!

Duncan

OFFER 1

How ready are you to open a venue?

We have created a checklist for you to find out!

It will help you identify the stages, timelines and actions that you need to consider before opening a hospitality venue.

**Download the free
HOSPITALITY CONCEPT
50-Point Checklist**

To download and complete,
simply SCAN QR CODE below

You can also visit
www.thecuttingedgeagency.com/resources

OFFER 2

Complimentary 30-Minute Call
'Discovery with Duncan'
Your roadmap from 'Vision to Creation'

- Have you always wanted to open your own hospitality venue be it a restaurant, café, bar or club?
- Are you worried that you don't have ALL the skills and are unsure how much it would cost?
- Have you been tasked with opening a venue and lack some of the knowhow of the process to follow?

This is your opportunity to spend the most valuable 30 minutes you have to invest in yourself and uncover a proven system that will give you the tools to jumpstart your new venture.

Don't fall into the trap others make when it comes to opening, running and growing a hospitality venue. As the saying goes, when you train you gain!!!

During this 30-minute discovery call, you will unlock:

- Your own unique customised 'Vision to Creation' roadmap
- The mistakes you must avoid as you start your journey
- The one money-saving hack that will help you get a head start on the competition.

This 'Discovery with Duncan' call is limited to just 10 sessions each month.

Please register for the **'DISCOVERY CALL'** at thecuttingedgeagency.com and select the the next available date for this unique opportunity.

You can view more information on our Hospitality Services as well access further resources and support for you and your team including:

- Concept Soul-utions
- Edge-ucation
- Sales-Edge
- Keynote Speaking
- Media, Blogs and Videos

Email us at info@thecuttingedgeagency.com
OR
Visit www.thecuttingedgeagency.com

DUNCAN FRASER-SMITH

Award Winning Hospitality Industry Expert
Speaker, Writer, Moderator, Panelist & Author

Duncan Fraser-Smith, a passionate accomplished Australian, boasts an impressive reputation as a dynamic innovator, disruptor and creator in the regional and international hospitality industry across the Middle East, Africa, Asia, Europe and Australia. He is the founder of The Cutting Edge Hospitality Agency.

- 30+ years experience creating restaurants, cafes, bars & clubs
- Over 200 hospitality concepts created worldwide including the world's first "MasterChef, the TV Experience" restaurant in Dubai
- Voted No1 Influencer in Caterer Middle East Power 50
- Voted 'Leading F&B Director' in Hotel & Catering News
- Founding Member of Global Restaurant Investment Forum (GRIF)
- Keynote Speaker, Moderator and panelist for International Trade Events
- Author of "CREATE TO PLATE"

KEY SPEAKER TOPICS

KEY DRIVERS TO CREATING CUTTING EDGE CONCEPTS
- Turning your emotion into motion
- How to trust your instincts at the right moments
- Planning to succeed rather than failing to plan

10 INGREDIENTS TO CONVERT YOUR VISION TO VENUE
- Roadmap of the 'Vision to Creation' model
- Creating innovative concepts that stand out in the marketplace
- Your dream customer unpacked

PASSION VS. PROFIT WHEN BUILDING YOUR DREAM VENUE
- Emotional intelligence when it comes to investing
- Discover the right and wrong places to allocate money
- Stay smart - stay on budget

📞 Australia +61 2 6190 9278   🌐 thecuttingedgeagency.com   ✉ duncan@thecuttingedgeagency.com
in duncanfrasersmith   f /thecuttingedgeagency   @ @duncanfs

RESOURCES

You may access and download all resources mentioned in the **ACTION** section at the end of each Chapter. Refer to Pages 22, 38, 55, 71 and 103.

Simply SCAN QR CODE below

Or visit

www.thecuttingedgeagency.com/resources

ABOUT THE AUTHOR

'I don't work. I spend my time doing what I love and if I can share just some of that with others, supporting them to grow through innovation, relevance, profitability AND be driven by their soul, then I have achieved my goal.'

Duncan Fraser-Smith

Duncan Fraser-Smith, is passionate, accomplished and boasts an impressive reputation as a dynamic innovator, disruptor and creator in the regional and international food and beverage scene. For over 30 years he has enjoyed success in key senior management roles within the hotel and restaurant industry across the Middle East, Asia, Europe and Australia working with the likes of Hyatt, IHG and Accor. He is also the founder of The Cutting Edge Hospitality Agency.

In 2008, Duncan left Australia and a progressive career in restaurant and bar operations, to take up his appointment as General Manager of Hospitality Operations at Doha Sports City, Qatar.

CREATE TO PLATE

Based in Dubai, UAE, since 2010 and voted the **No.1 Influencer** In Caterer Middle East 'POWER 50', his journey began as Group Director of Design, Food and Beverage for InterContinental Hotels Group (IHG) creating and developing numerous food and beverage concepts for the group across the Middle East, Europe, Africa and Asia.

In 2013, Duncan founded The Cutting Edge Hospitality Agency and was involved in some of the region's most dynamic projects. He was instrumental in bringing acclaimed Michelin starred chef Jason Atherton to open Marina Social in Dubai. He led the launch of Clé Restaurant and Bar with Michelin starred chef Greg Malouf and executed one of Dubai's most high-profile openings. He crafted the unique Intersect by Lexus concept, the second to open worldwide and worked hand in hand with Michelin starred chef Pierre Gagnaire to create and launch Choix Patisserie to name a few.

Duncan's entrepreneurial spirit also led him to create a preferred partnership with Banijay Group (formerly Endemol Shine) the TV production company behind the MasterChef reality TV series to successfully launch 'MasterChef, the TV Experience' a world-first 'screen to plate' restaurant concept that embodies the emotional connection found between the consumer and MasterChef champions from across the globe.

His contribution is highly sought after and well respected and he has been involved in the creation of over 200 hospitality concepts globally. Duncan is an expert operator, keynote speaker, forum moderator, panelist, author and a contributing writer for some of the world's leading industry publications.

ABOUT THE AUTHOR

His passion, vision, innovation and collaboration has brought many new hospitality concepts and brands to life, and is an indication of his commitment to continually contribute to the evolution, growth and development of the industry that he loves.

www.ingramcontent.com/pod-product-compliance
Lightning Source LLC
Chambersburg PA
CBHW030300100526
44590CB00012B/462